W9-AXU-358

The Church and the
Amateur Adult

+

THE KNUBEL-MILLER LECTURES — 1955

The Church and the Amateur Adult

By
Ralph W. Loew

BOARD OF PUBLICATION
OF THE UNITED LUTHERAN CHURCH IN AMERICA
PHILADELPHIA

© 1955, BY MUHLENBERG PRESS

Library of Congress Catalog
Card Number 55-11780

Printed in U.S.A.

To the promising young Christians in our household

CAROLYN and JANET

That they may grow in grace and in favor with God and man

Foreword

The assignment of the subject, *After Confirmation, What?* by the Knubel-Miller Founder is the ready recognition that the church is concerned that confirmation be no graduation ceremony. Its retention as a necessary rite is universally recognized. What the church desires is continuing interest in and development of a growth and maturity in Christian thinking and living. We know that it has to be more than ceremony and memorization with a dash of ethical teaching.

For this book, the title *The Church and the Amateur Adult* has been selected simply because young people must be treated as adults, although in some cases they have not matured to that area of confidence where they can manage life's problems with certainty. It must be the concern of the church to help these young people grow in faith to the point where they are able to make the decisive moral judgments required by life.

These lectures are not set forth as psychological studies nor as the development of plans and programs. They are some reactions of a pastor who writes from the vantage point of the regular work and program of parish life.

These papers are written in the belief that young people are persons, that they belong to the whole community of the church, that they are maturing in this fast-moving age with a growing sense of stability for their idealism and some goals for their restlessness. They constitute the continuing hope of the church. I have seen them confront calls to mission fields, watched them take a sense of dedication into their careers, listened to them discuss their hopes and dreams, and have hoped that their elders might be as honest in confronting the challenge to mind and heart.

These then are meant to be practical statements which grew out of the overflow of gladness for the challenge of pastoral work, illustrated especially in a concern for the ongoing, maturing Christian life. "Stir up the gift that is in thee."

There are many technical books in this field and the bibliography of special writings in the area of young people's problems is a long one.

Any acknowledgment of indebtedness would include a long list of valued friends. I especially want to mention those congregations where I have had the privilege of serving, and where I have known maturing young Christians who have eagerly searched for a relevant and vigorous faith: The Lutheran Parish of Millersburg, Ohio; Reformation Lutheran Church, Washington, D. C.; and Holy Trinity Lutheran Church, Buffalo, N. Y. Dr. Gould Wickey, Executive Secretary, Board of Higher Education, has been of inestimable value in generously sharing guidance in the preparation of these lectures. Likewise, the dedicated leaders of the Board of Parish Education, and of the Luther League of America, all of the United Lutheran Church in America, have been of value beyond measure.

Buffalo, N. Y.   RALPH W. LOEW
June 1955

Table of Contents

I

The End of the Beginning

The Father in Heaven, for Jesus' sake, renew and increase in thee the gift of the Holy Ghost,

+

A few years ago in Washington, D. C., a young man sat before me discussing his problems of loneliness and frustration. Suddenly, he asked, "Have you ever been in a barrel of custard?" I confessed I'd never even imagined such a thing. Then he added, "I feel that I'm in over my head and yet I can't get hold of anything." To many persons any discussion of the problems of the church and young people is of the same general pattern. Everyone recognizes the need; few suggest the answers. Somewhere we must achieve that answer in our time. Said Alfred Noyes, "There is an overwhelming body of truth in the intellectual armories of Christendom which has only to be rightly used to ensure a change of heart and mind throughout the world." This tapping of the resources and discovering the way of relating this truth to a growing awareness is one of our foremost responsibilities.

There must be an increasing interest in a discovery of spiritual resources. "Today our best plans miscarry because they are in the hands of people who have undergone no further growth," said Lewis Mumford. "Most of these people have shrunk from facing the world crisis, and they have no notion of the manner in which they themselves have helped to bring it about. Into every new situation they carry only a fossilized self. Their hidden prejudices, their glib hopes, their archaic desires and automatisms usually couched in the language of assertive modernity, recall those of the fourth century, B.C. or the Romans of the fourth century A.D. They are in a power dive and their controls have frozen. By closing their eyes they think they can avoid a crash." [1] This is the all-too-frequent psychological pattern of thought and action in our time.

There is still a considerable number of persons who are within our churches; in fact, the number is greater than ever in history. More persons attend services of worship, contribute more dollars, share in more activities and in many ways express a sincere and devout interest in the maintenance and continuance of their religious institutions. One of the speakers at the second Assembly of the World Council of Churches used such statistics to prove that we are a "responsible society." He indicated the generous gifts poured out by Christians in this nation, declaring those as symbols of religious health. That may be true, but we can come close to the Pharisee in his boasting of his tithes and fastings. There must be other standards indicating religious health.

It is just at this place that men recognize their problem in passing on truth to another generation. Former Chancellor Hutchins of the University of Chicago once pointed out that communication is society's basic problem. Ours is the difficulty of articulating our faith, stating it in terms which are significant and relevant to another generation.

Either we shall succeed in this challenge or we shall lose the battle in this margin of time. Someone has pointed out that if the whole earth were Christian that condition would only last until

[1] Lewis Mumford, *The Condition of Man* (New York: Harcourt, 1944), p. 422.

the next baby was born. We are always only a generation or so from extinction. The processes of education are ever challenging.

So, "the idea conceived and born by the passion of one heart can shape and change the life of millions, leading great nations on to destruction or destiny. We have seen it happen more than once in our own lifetime.

"Ideas are on the march today. Ideas move faster than armies. They travel ahead of them as well as behind them. They need no ships to cross the seas, neither will fortifications keep them behind frontiers.

"Ideas to transform history are bidding for the hearts of all humanity today. There is the idea that one class should dominate, and that one section should dominate, or that one race should dominate, or that one group of nations should dominate.

"Yet in the end, all these ideas will fail for there is one idea destined to master all others in this day and age—to establish in our lifetime the fresh, brave world for which all openly long and in which few wholeheartedly believe." [2]

One of the treasured traditions of the Lutheran church has been in its catechetical training and its rite of confirmation. The needs of succeeding generations have been met, at least in part, by this evolving pattern of an educational approach to a maturing faith. Each generation will bring its diversities in training, in method and in approach. The treasure remains.

Lutheran pastors regard this teaching responsibility as one of the privileges of the week. Our problem is that the rite of confirmation is regarded popularly as a graduating service, the completion of the training. Most of us know that this isn't what we want or plan. In the busy schedules of the overworked pastor with a deluge of meetings, calls, and events, matched against the equally busy schedule of growing and active young people, it

[2] Peter Howard, *Ideas Have Legs* (New York: Coward-McCann, 1946), p. 3.

becomes increasingly difficult to continue the processes of educational growth and a maturing faith.

This series of papers suggests no easy methods, five bits of calisthenics and all's well! There are too many diverse situations, and community life is too complicated for that. There are some forthright principles which need emphasis, and these must be applied, amended, adapted, developed in the varying situations in which the church is at work.

Our generation is aware of the need of reaching young people with the challenge to rethink the heritage of their fathers in the terms of their own particular environment. "The young persons of today, growing up as they have had to in the midst of an adult generation in turmoil and with a war and military service in the offing, can hardly be blamed for a lack of consistent moral ideas and a settled purpose. During the same period . . . the tendency in both secondary and higher education to subordinate liberal technical culture to technical skills has left many with more of such skills than with moral incentives for using them." [3]

This is the challenge confronting the honest church which desires to reach its young people not by force or ceremonies or traditions, but rather to "rekindle the gift of God that is within you through the laying on of hands; for God did not give us a spirit of timidity, but a spirit of power and love and self-control." [4]

THE CHURCH AND CATECHETICAL INSTRUCTION

For most of our churches confirmation means the culmination of a period of training for young people preparatory to active participation in the life of the church. For all of the individuality of our parish life, there is a surprising unanimity in procedure. Reports indicate that 55% of the congregations of the United

[3] Georgia Harkness, *The Sources of Western Morality* (New York: Scribners, 1955).
[4] II Timothy 1:6-7 (R.S.V.).

Lutheran Church in America require two years of catechetical study, usually conducted by the pastor, preparatory for confirmation. Five per cent of the United Lutheran congregations require three years of such study. There is a very definite trend in favor of enrolling all seventh-grade students or twelve-year-old children in such a preparatory class. A poll of the Lutheran church in America would reveal a unanimous vote in favor of continuing catechetical procedure in spite of the problems of maintaining these classes in the complicated urban and educational patterns of our time. This training resembles the closing of a sluice gate in a canal whereby the water level can be raised to permit the ship to proceed. We know that we have to reach higher levels. The problem arises in our assuring young people that the journey must continue. We have to get the ship out into the deeper waters.

The textbook for this work has been Luther's Small Catechism. Published in 1529, it was originally intended as a brief summary of the Christian faith. Before long, it was a textbook and, with the spread of the Reformation, it became a central factor in religious education in home and church. "It became the textbook in every Lutheran land and wherever Lutherans left their homeland, the Catechism went along. Campanius sought to teach it to the Indians in Pennsylvania; Muhlenberg brought out an English translation published in Germantown. The Scandinavians brought their Catechism with them and it became the textbook in the parochial schools of the Missouri Synod congregations." As a matter of fact, most pastors know of members who report that they can quote the catechism in the language of their fathers. This became the symbol of their historical continuity, the brief succinct statements which became the sum and substance of the faith that is within them. There is no inconsiderable heritage for, in a time when religion is represented in so many confused and sentimental patterns, it is of some significance to have available this heritage of an elemental foundation.

In an address before the Ministerium of Pennsylvania, Dr. Conrad Bergendoff asserted, "Indeed the history of religious education in the American Lutheran Synods is largely the story of the ways and places and language in which the doctrines of the Catechism were taught. When we honor the educators of the Lutheran church in America, it is not enough to go back to 1748 or 1738. We must go back to 1529 and to Luther's concept of religious education." [5]

This recognition places the catechism at the very heart of the educational life of the church, saving it from maudlin sentimentalism or simply a class in ethics. "Luther's Catechism gives us a good guide as to what knowledge is essentially the good life and the conscience; why we still have a right to talk with God, even though we are sinful; how we should speak with God; who God is, and what he has done; how God calls us wicked people to be his children and washes us clean. Foremost is the story of the Paschal bread and wine and how Jesus linked them to his living, dying and rising in power." [6] To quote Gustav Wiencke, "In crisp brevity, in easy rhythm of language, in a feeling for what is concrete and essential, Luther's Catechism has never been excelled. A good parish priest could have set up a catechism suitable for Saxon peasants, but it took evangelical insight of Luther to make the catechism a witness and key to the Christian faith which was to transcend his century and his age." [7]

Martin Luther himself said of the Catechism, "The Catechism is the true lay-Bible containing the whole Christian teaching as each Christian must know it for his spiritual blessedness. The Catechism contains the best and most perfect teaching. Therefore it should be preached again and again without ceasing, and all the common preaching should be founded upon it and related

---

[5] Conrad Bergendoff, *The Lutheran Church in Higher Education.*
[6] George Arbaugh, *The Growth of a Christian* (Philadelphia: Muhlenberg Press, 1953).
[7] Gustav Wiencke, "Confirmation Instruction in Historical Perspective," *Lutheran Quarterly*, VII (1955), p. 107.

to it. I wish men would preach it every day and simply read it from the book." [8]

To do this would be no dull business. It would save us all from a shoddy cheapness. For to preach it and teach it in the setting of our environment and with the vigorous relevancy that Luther himself was forever exhibiting might save us from the perils of inanity as well as the boredom of just restating acceptable cliches.

Several things are obvious in the history of this instruction through the generation of recorded spiritual history.

1. *The Church Has Always Been Concerned That Its Youth Be Taught.*

The Jewish system of education which came to its height in the period between 70 B.C and A.D. 85 compelled children to attend school at the age of 7 years. The school was held in the synagogue or in a separate building. The children repeated the words of the sacred writings; they memorized the traditions of their people and they were reared in the laws and the sacred sayings.

Throughout Christian history, instruction was associated with baptism; with instruction of the new catechumens and leading them into a knowledge of the faith. Luther's concern was precisely at this point, namely, with the ignorance of the people, with the superstition of his generation, with the fears which were ingrained and the tired intellectualism, with the willingness to escape responsibility. This was the springboard for his writing.

2. *The Methods of Instruction Have Changed Throughout the Centuries.*

In the early church, doctrine was preserved and the life of the believers protected by admitting to baptism only those who

[8] Martin Luther in *Day by Day We Magnify Thee* (Philadelphia: Muhlenberg Press, 1950), p. 377.

had been provided with special schools set up by the bishop. The catechumens were admitted only to the preaching services and special acts of consecration admitted the hearers to the prayers of the church.

Not until just before the baptism were the words of the Creed revealed and the catechumens were received by the laying on of hands and exorcism. Following a rigorous period of prayer, fasting, confession of sins, they were solemnly baptized and admitted to the holy Eucharist.

As the church grew, whole villages were received into the membership of the church, and baptism preceded the act of confirmation or consecration. Gradually confirmation became an act of admission without instruction. By Luther's time, the four parts of catechetical instruction, where followed, were the Lord's Prayer, the Ave Maria, Apostles' Creed and the Decalog. The method most frequently used was simple memorization. Any of us will remember hearing faithful members tell of the days in which they memorized the entire catechism and usually in some foreign tongue. The class period was made up of lecture and question and answer period. Trotzendorff (1556), who was regarded as a very accomplished teacher, defined a catechist as a teacher who repeats orally what is to be learned so often that the pupil can repeat it after him.

The modern discussional methods, the history of a variety of catechetical instruction books in this century ranging from Stump's Catechism to the various workbooks and methods of instruction used in our own time, such as Nolde, Irvin and others, indicate the need of regarding confirmation instruction as no rigid form.

3. *There Has Been Little Precedent for the Problem of Instruction Confronted in America.*

The ancient church thought of catechetical instruction as a

major educational matter. In the development of the life of homogeneous states and communities in Europe, catechetical instruction was considered a responsibility of the church, but it was also a part of the regular program. Luther did not necessarily think of his catechism in the way it is used today. It was for him an instructional booklet to be used by the parish priest and the home. These two centers of influence became the important foci for the communication of the faith.

In America, in the earliest periods of our history, this use of the Catechism and the instruction of children was a chief responsibility of the church, and antedates the development of the public schools. The complicated urban structure of our society today, the problem created by the mobility of population, the difficulties encountered in reaching young people—all have enormously complicated the problem.

There was a time when such catechetical instruction was regarded as the accepted procedure. Now, the diverse practices of Protestant groups make it especially difficult to maintain these long periods of instruction within the churches which believe in this type of educational procedure.

Likewise, there may be a desire on the part of many pastors to hold confirmation at a later age than that of 14 years, which is the most accepted period. Defying him at this point is the competition for time which is presented by the educational and social schedules of every family and community. Almost everyone laments juvenile delinquency and at the same time defies the institutions that try to establish any kind of religious education within the home. We are willing to contribute funds or blame one aspect or another of society for the conditions in which we find ourselves, but we are loathe to imitate that which we seem to be willing to subsidize. As Elton Trueblood recently indicated, "Personal happiness must never become our chief end or goal [within the family]. The purpose is not to be happy but to perpetuate what is best for human life. Of course, happiness usually comes in such a procedure but it comes as a by-product." [9]

This means that the continuance and strengthening of confirmation instruction in the American scene presents increasing difficulties which have to be understood and met. The most agreed-upon age in meeting this problem of competing schedules of much-sought-after young people is simply to reach them in that period of primary adolescence, namely 12 to 15 years of age. That's a difficult time of life, but perhaps as good a time as any to rekindle the faith. Phyllis McGinley portrays the unsettled condition of this age in the enlightening grasp of confusion, entitled:

PORTRAIT OF GIRL WITH COMIC BOOK

Thirteen's no age at all. Thirteen is nothing,
It is not wit, or powder on the face,
Or Wednesday matinees, or misses' clothing,
Or intellect, or grace.
Twelve has its tribal customs. But thirteen
Is neither boys in battered cars or dolls
Nor Sara Crewe, or movie magazine,
Or pennants on the walls.

Thirteen keeps diaries and tropical fish
A month, at most; scorns jump ropes in the Spring;
Could not, would fortune grant it, name its wish;
Wants nothing, everything;
Has secrets from itself, friends it despises;
Admits none to the terrors that it feels;
Owns half a mask but no disguises;
And walks upon its heels.

Thirteen's anomalous—not that, not this
Not folded bud, or wave that laps a shore
Or moth proverbial from the Chrysalis.

[9] Elton Trueblood, *The Recovery of Family Life* (New York: Harper, 1953), p. 49.

Is the one age defeats the metaphor.
Is not a town, like childhood, strongly walled
But easily surrounded; is no city.
Nor, quitted once, can it be quite recalled—
Not even with pity.[10]

(I read this copy to my own thirteen-year-old daughter and she, listening attentively, said, "I don't get it.")

Yet with all of these significant problems, the church is intent on strengthening this important contribution of our faith to our generation. When the pastor repeats that ancient formula, "The Father in Heaven, for Jesus' sake, renew and increase in thee the gift of the Holy Ghost," he is announcing a faith for the continuing witness to the presence of God. To regard this as a moment of finality or of a placing of an indelible stamp on life is to misuse the rite. It marches against all that we know of God's witnessing spirit as he calls, gathers, enlightens and sanctifies his church.

So, this is our problem. We have made confirmation an event, much like graduation. We have placed robes on these young people, evolved dignified ceremonies, given gifts, and done those things which have been of significance to growing young people who are received into the membership of the church. All of this is of significance and needs to be preserved. But it needs to be the door, not the end of the road; the end of the beginning.

The danger of our indoctrination is simply that we may seem to mean conformation, the hemming and hedging of minds into narrow patterns. Young people are conformists in many ways. The aim of catechetical instruction is to give young people a basis whereby they can grow and develop a mature faith; whereby they can become explorers. Or, to use the words of Dr. Reu,[11]

---

[10] Phyllis McGinley, *Love Letters* (New York: Viking, 1954), p. 11. Copyright 1952, 1954, by Phyllis McGinley. Originally published in *The New Yorker*.

[11] Johann M. Reu, *Catechetics* (Chicago: Wartburg, 1918), p. 306.

11

"Here I learn how to become a child of God and how I remain one." That "remaining" is not static—it is dynamic.

Here is the recognition of the validity of baptism, the renewing and increasing of faith. We need to state carefully in our time what we expect of the newly confirmed. Ideally, these young people have become a part of the church. They are now recognized as "communing members," persons prepared to receive the sacraments and participate in the life of the church.

The fact of the matter is that this presents a problem to both young persons and the church. The church is the universal company of believers, which includes these newest members of this family. It is a rarified atmosphere, if it were to be fully recognized. The truth is that for many of these newly confirmed, it is very much as it was the week before—the church of their fathers. It has to be their church, and it must be this personalizing of a relationship, this development of faith as the lifeblood instead of a badge; the corpuscles instead of an amulet; the stuff of life instead of something new to be sustained. To all too many of these young people, the church seems to be one more institution thrust upon their already too crowded schedules.

ASSUMPTIONS ABOUT CONFIRMATION

If we are to learn from the history of this experience of training which has been the just pride of the church, there are at least eleven definite assumptions which need to be emphasized.

1. *We are celebrating a rite, a custom, an act which validates or newly confirms the fact of baptism.* Confirmation is not a sacrament. It is a step and only one important step, in the maturing of the Christian faith. It ends a kind of preparing for a new church experience. Have we made it too symbolic, too final in its form?

2. Confirmation *demands that we establish such large concepts that a growing mind cannot outgrow his faith.* We have abused

a privilege if we give young people too small a concept of God; too parochial a concept of faith; too rigid a pattern of life. God's vastness has been made known to us in Jesus Christ, his infinity has been known to us in a world of the finite. Our teaching and experience must be filled with this greatness known in the everyday acts of life. Sometimes we shall have done more for them if we have companioned them in reading Scripture, praying with them and unfolding to them the adventure of Christian living. Many a parent has purchased clothing for a youngster in a size too large with the pious hope that "he'll grow into it." We need to do that with our concepts of faith, clothing them now, allowing them to grow—to stretch intellectually, and to find themselves still warmed and garbed in their maturing life.

"The teacher of religion is bound to keep in mind that the church is the communion of true believers, and that the children entrusted to him are in truth members of it only when they have attained to personal faith and, as corollary thereto, to participation in all privileges and duties of the mature congregation; and he will choose all his educational and disciplinary measures with a view to the goal to which God unquestionably some time means to lead the soul. But when he is asked to define the aim of his own educational efforts, he will, in humility, answer as follows: The aim is (1) faithfully to imbed and anchor in the INTELLECT of the rising generation all the holy truths upon which the life of the mature congregation fundamentally is based, and by which alone it is constantly renewed, and without a knowledge of which one cannot possibly participate in its entire life; (2) to stir the EMOTIONS to a vital interest in those truths; (3) to bend the WILL so that it may run in the paths in which the Holy Spirit, turning to account those truths, in his own season, leads to personal faith and to participate in the life of the mature congregation." [12]

[12] *Ibid.*, p. 312.

3. *The local congregation must be prepared to become an incarnation of this growing faith.* The experience of confirmation is not a discipline to be gotten through and forgotten; it is the end of the preliminary preparation for a growing, maturing faith. What has been done has been elemental. Now there is an active sharing of mind and spirit. It is this point at which the church must be large enough in its thinking, and adventurous enough in its faith to challenge these growing minds. We must prepare the organizational structure of the church to receive these amateur adults.

4. *Confirmation is the willing testimonial that the religious life is the educable life.* That does not mean that it becomes an intellectual discipline, a single memorizing of facts, no matter how important these facts may be. It also implies the education of the emotions, the development of a feeling for life, the thinking upon those things which St. Paul noted: "those things which are true, just, pure, lovely, and of good report." It is our most important venture now.

5. *Confirmation ought to produce young people better able to discuss their faith* and to become articulate in a challenging world. As we shall see, these young people are whisked into a world where the consequences of believing are increasingly challenging. Until this moment, it is assumed that these young people have been encouraged in believing, have been nurtured in faith, have been strengthened by fellowship. They may now wrongly assume that this is the way it is in this world. They will soon discover the sheer risk of faith, the fact that in this world some men die for their faith. Our class procedures and the concurrent experiences of the class instructions ought to encourage this discussion of faith. Luther translated the essentials of Scripture into the simplest language; it is our challenge to translate the articles of faith into a language relevant to today's events. We are not just to memorize; we are engaged in the

adventure of the renewal and increasing of faith.[13] "To expect a child to use the language of the mature Christian is to produce a race of prigs, for a prig is a person whose attitude is out of keeping with his sensibility. And priggishness is the negation of Christian excellence."

6. *Confirmation requires an understanding of the experience of worship wherein it is a willing sharing.* These young people live in a world of varying liturgical experiences, a complex of expressions of worship. They need to understand what they are doing, and why they are doing it, namely, the historical backgrounds, the intellectual content and the emotional purpose. We know that the novelty of kneeling once at the communion rail needs now to become the ever new experience of God's forgiving love. The self-conscious presence at the Lord's Supper needs to be matured into the meeting of the Real Presence of Christ. In a recent volume, Dr. Shoemaker deplored the contentment of many persons with pretending, play-acting, putting on the externals of religion and being satisfied. This dressing up, as though this were church, he contends, is no substitute for a renewal and increase of faith. His strictures on the Episcopal church are as cogent for the Lutheran.[14]

7. *These young people have been reared in a denominational pattern quite unlike the experiences of the early Reformers, and quite unlike almost any other experience in Christian history.* They are thrust into a world where the confusion of life is increasingly apparent. Furthermore, they live in that world in their maturing experience. They know that the world is not just made up of Lutherans. Their social relationships, their experience in daily life, especially in the vastly changing life of most areas of our countries, drive that factor home day after day. We

[13] See A. Victor Murray, *Education Into Religion* (New York: Harper, 1953), p. 18.
[14] Samuel Shoemaker, *By the Power of God* (New York: Harper, 1954), pp. 98-99.

have to build an appreciation, the message of the Lutheran church to this generation, and at the same time understand that we are not just schooling young people in denominational loyalty. We are praying for the renewal and increase of the gift of the Holy Spirit. We are preparing to risk maturing young people who are adequately prepared, wanting them to make their choices as Christians and to abide by them.

8. *Confirmation is a complement to the patterns and habits of the home, not a substitute.* All too many of us are acquainted with the parents who tell us at the beginning of a catechetical period that they have looked forward to confirmation as a time when the pastor could do what they as parents hadn't been able to do. The pastor is not a substitute parent. He is a guide, a teacher, a friend, a leader, and if he is of the very best, he will be one who steps down the high voltage of Christian truth to the level of these young people with the wise gifts of an enthusiastic personality and friendship. The gifts of the Holy Ghost are gifts to the total personality. Catechetical instruction, if it is to presume something after confirmation, presupposes a home willing to co-operate and understanding that what goes on in the confines of the church reaches into the habits of life and the understanding of the family circle. Confirmation procedures require precatechetical conferences of parents and pastor in arriving at a common understanding of what is the aim of such instruction. If there ever was a time when it could be automatically assumed that the home would understand the aims of catechetical instruction, that time is not now. The chaos of much urban and rural life demands a new rapport between pastor and home.

To Luther, "The life of the family was a mask of God to both parents and children. To children, for through their parents God had created them and in the parents God called for their reverence and respect. To parents, too, for in their children they faced a sacred responsibility and a divine opportunity for service. Luther had only exquisite scorn for the professional do-gooders of his day, who were perfectly willing to do something for the good of society and for the church, but who shunned the duty and responsibility of parenthood, by which they could have best served both society and the church. He said that the sight of one child reared for God should put all monks to shame. Yet many parents were neglecting this responsibility, so that 'One fool trains another, and as they have lived, so their children live after them.' " [15]

9. *Confirmation ought to prepare young people for a relaxed healthiness in confronting the problems of growing up.* This period of the young adult, (13 to 21 years of age) is no easy time. The normal tensions and insecurities are not erased by any period of training. What can happen is the laying of the necessary foundations, the acquaintance with resources of power, the establishment of enduring friendships, the introduction into habits which inspire patience, the opening of life for the inpouring of these gifts of the Holy Ghost. What these young people instinctively know is that something is going to possess them. They give themselves to organizations, to things, to groups. Wrote Dr. Reinhold Niebuhr in the Gifford Lectures, "The self knows the world, insofar as it knows the world, because it stands outside both itself and the world, which means that it cannot understand itself except as it is understood from beyond self and the world . . . for the world which stands outside itself and the world cannot find the meaning of life in itself or the world. Human personality is so constructed that it must be possessed if it is to escape the prison of self-possession. Self-possession means self-interestedness. The self must be possessed from beyond itself."

It is this which is the ambition of all rightful catechetical instruction. This is a far larger pattern than just memorizing, disciplining or initiating. It is doing all of these things, plus. It

[15] Jaroslav Pelikan, *Fools for Christ* (Philadelphia: Muhlenberg Press, 1955), p. 108.

is teaching, plus. It is guiding, plus. That plus is the opening of life to the greatness of the Christian cause in the whole of existence. When it does this, it ought to create that quality of relaxed healthiness which is the symbol of a normal young person who has found security, satisfaction and affection in life.

10. *The fellowship of the Holy Spirit is in the church, which is symbolized but not bounded by the local congregation.* Confirmation is not a promise to abide in one spot. It is the beginning of a relationship to the whole of the Christian church through the local congregation. It is a relationship to the widespread programs of the church and a fellowship with the workings of the Holy Spirit in the multiform activities of Christendom everywhere. "Christianity means community through Jesus Christ. It is no more or less than this. Whether it be a brief encounter or a daily fellowship of the years, Christian community is only this. We belong to one another because we belong to Christ." [16]

Parochialism has always been dangerous and never more so than now. There is no keeping of young persons anchored to one spot, one geographical setting, one place. They live in the midst of exploding communities, atomized social structures. If a young person is bound north, south, east, and west by his congregation, then, strong as his personal congregational loyalty has been, the new and luring experience of the future will be a disturbing one.

This is not to disturb our sense of the importance of local congregations. It is rather understanding the importance of the body without underrating the fact that we belong to humanity. It is the congregation as a place in the church. It is the plea of Paul, "I beseech you, therefore, brethren, that ye present your bodies [your congregational loyalties] as a living sacrifice . . . which is your reasonable service."

To put that point into the thinking and appreciation of young

[16] Dietrich Bonhoeffer, *Life Together* (New York: Harper, 1954), p. 21.

people at the time when there is a chance to deal with them in terms of belonging to the whole of the church is of utmost importance.

11. *Confirmation introduces young people into the fellowship of the church where their idealism meets the experience and the enthusiasm of the members as well as the selfishness, the traditional bonds and the rigidity of many who have lost the fervor of their confirmation.* The whole business of confirmation can end at that point, with little renewing or increasing, unless young people know that the church has many persons who are nominally members but who have long since taken to subsidizing that which they would never imitate.

There are the people who expect their pastor to preach in favor of racial understanding but have no intention of doing so themselves. There is the churchman who has sanctified all of the old without understanding that it can be the seedbed of the new. There are the idolators who have mistaken a prejudice for a conviction. These folks are by and large their own parents or friends. This is the Christian church exemplified in one congregation.

"Pentecost is normal Christianity. It is normal to have people's lives so invaded by the Power of God that they are lifted out of themselves into another kind of life in Christ. It is normal to have the fire and stirring excitement that were in the early church." [17]

We are preparing Christian young people for the business of living Christian lives. This is not a race to see how much we can memorize, or digest, but a thoroughgoing, disciplined fellowship which is the first step in developing enthusiastic Christian living. This is what we want of our newly confirmed. How they shall express this Christian witness and enthusiasm is the adventure that yet remains. What we expect of them is a pattern for the

[17] *Ibid.*, p. 21.

expression of life, the development of those attitudes which can hold them across the years. We want them to know that "to live in a world where Christ is risen is to live in a world where Christ is our contemporary." [18]

A pastor once told the poignant story of the young wife whose husband was overseas who each night tucked their little youngster into bed with a prayer and a good night story. Then the little fellow would go across the room, kiss the picture of his daddy and tumble into bed. This went on for some months until the inevitable day dawned when the father came home. The little fellow eyed this stranger who had come into the household and disrupted routines. He knew that this stranger was related to him, but he had no notion of what they should do with each other. After the evening meal, the little fellow was ready for bed. This night the father came along to the bedroom and the mother said, "Now, son, this is the night when you don't have to kiss the picture. You can kiss your Daddy." The little fellow eyed his father, looked at the picture, ran across the room, kissed the picture and tumbled into bed.

This pathetic story is a perfect example of that which happens in our Christian living. We have become so accustomed to the framed picture of religion that we miss the voice of our Heavenly Father. We are more accustomed to a semblance of something than to the thing itself. Whenever we have prepared Christian young people for participation in the life of the church, it is to introduce them to the lure of the renewal of faith, the gifts of the Holy Ghost coming afresh, being renewed and rethought and relived. The pattern of reality needs to be set day after day until life can be seen steadily and whole. This is the achievement of the Christian whose life is unified by the gospel, and who searches for truth through facts and information, as well as through inspiration.

[18] D. T. Niles, *That They May Have Life* (New York: Harper, 1951), p. 26.

At the time of confirmation, the young person ought to have developed a pattern of worship, to have been introduced into the storehouse of faith, to have been given a desire for a growing faith, to have established patterns of personal and corporate worship and to have arrived at a friendship with great thinkers and personalities who have lived in a conscious knowledge of God's search for the human personality. Here we are at the heart of our ambition for the newly confirmed. A process of education has intensified the awakened search for truth. It is the end of the beginning, the adventure of the amateur adult in the search for "the high calling of God in Christ Jesus."

SOME SUGGESTIONS FROM OTHERS

One pastor reports that he gives a period of training at the age of 14 years (or 8th grade), preparing for the reception of Holy Communion. Young people are admitted to communion at this age, with confirmation classes being continued until age 18 (or 12th grade) at which time the rite of confirmation is celebrated.

One church reports a series of field trips and discussion periods following confirmation. The class goes as a group to social agencies and churches of other affiliations, discussing observations and providing the opportunity for continuing catechetical discussion in a different context.

One church reports a structure in congregational organization in which the church councilmen or deacons become the chairmen of larger congregational committees. Thus the Committees on Evangelism, Stewardship, Education, etc., have newly confirmed members, as well as men and women of maturity, working together.

II

Pressures on the Amateur Adult

To Thy Strengthening in Faith

+

After the second Comet explosion over the Mediterranean some months ago, the British experts cancelled all flights and began a study of the causes of the disasters. Recently the results were announced and the finger of accusation was pointed to what experts called metal fatigue.

A scientific footnote explained that this isn't failure of metal after repeated straining. Small cracks which sometimes start as tool marks, sharp indentations or other stress raisers, spread through the metal until it breaks. Sufficient strength, correct design and careful fabrication prevent such failures. *Time* magazine reports that the designers are busily at work attempting to correct the fabrication of the planes in order that there be no repetition of these disasters.

The fascinating element revealed in this incident is in the significance of the seemingly insignificant. A metal scratch, a small indentation, a slight fracture, and the explosion of a great plane results. Left on the ground, the scratch was nothing, or so it seemed. The stresses and strain built up when the plane is flying at terrific speeds 40,000 feet above the earth cause that little defect to become the mark of tragedy.

So science underscores the insights of the theologian. The fatal "scratch" in the human make-up cannot be so easily overlooked. We have tried "urbanity, individualism, humanism, intelligence," and, for all of our altruistic efforts we are still confronted with an incompetence in handling life situations. When the pace is fast, and it is increasingly so, pressures are built up which cause the disintegration of personality. It is this which has affected the make-up of the society in which we live. The children confirmed into the church are not protected from the heat and passion of the world. They are sent into the world after an experience in which some fundamental groundwork has been laid, and they are now to meet the pressures with the skill and insight of adults. In truth, they are amateur adults, adults because they are growing, but amateurs or apprentices inasmuch as they are still in a maturing process which will take many years to complete.

The week after confirmation, a young person needs to be strengthened in faith. The Word must come into new flesh and the gospel find expression in a new life. It is just at this point that the church faces an important challenge. The emotional experience of confirmation needs now to be buttressed by a resolute faith, resilient enough to meet the pressures which are quite suddenly confronted. He has to make decisions, many of them irrevocable ones, making them in our time much earlier than they have been made in the past quarter of a century. Younger marriages, the necessity of determining professional choices, the mobility of population, the competition for social recognition are all the battering pressures which are exerted upon the young peoples of our parishes who look to us for friendship, for guidance and for assistance. Perhaps one of the problems younger people have is that they're supposed to have problems. Sometimes they may think they have to live up to an unhappy standard. As a matter of fact, every church knows that there are thousands upon thousands of younger men and women who desire only to emulate that description of Jesus, to grow "in wisdom and in stature and in favor with God and man." (After all, some middle-aged folk produce some of the most monumental problems that dwarf teen-age difficulties.)

> Youth awaits leadership.
> Youth seeks the fuller life.
> Youth needs to be commanded.
> Youth dreams, hopes, dares.
> Youth will follow someone.
> Youth will be devoted to something—
>> But
> Who will provide that leadership?
> How will youth find the fuller life?
> Who will command youth?
> Will the dreams and hopes of youth lead him forward with God or not?
> Will youth dare to be Christian?
> Who will lead youth—Christ or the foes of the lesser life?
> Who will help youth find those devotions which are worthy of the loyalty of all mankind?
> These are the concerns of the church and the leaders of youth.[1]

JESUS AND AMATEUR ADULTS

Among the instances recorded in Scripture are three notable experiences in which Jesus dealt with amateur adults. The first is the prodigal son, a startling example of the clash between the generations, the problems of a displaced young man. This amateur adult, who believed he had been wronged because he had not been understood, demanded that which was not his own. And got it. The story of this young man's clash with his father is as contemporary as the events of our own time. It arises from the same springs of action as the clash with family schedules, the competition for things, the need for more finances, a car or some other necessity of social approval which is in current society.

[1] Roy Burkhart, *Understanding Youth* (Nashville: Abingdon, 1952), p. 34.

Psychology indicates that there are four wishes which we all have: recognition from others; affectionate response from them; security and a feeling of at-homeness in our situation; experiences that are fresh, vital and novel enough to rescue us from stagnation and boredom. If we are locked from legitimate fulfilment of these desires we are unhappy and dissatisfied. If we find a proper fulfilment, we can live in reasonable happiness and usefulness.

The prodigal son was obviously a person who was at odds with his situation, who couldn't tolerate the reality of an existence at home and who dreamed often of an escape into an exciting new adventure. The escape was one from security to a bold departure. It is in such a moment that the church has to confront the young people whom it can reach. The truth is, for that matter, that many young people believe, rightly or wrongly, that they cannot talk with their parents, or that their parents will not understand. What's more, there is no inheritance which they can demand, nothing which can be appropriated which would make escape possible. They feel trapped and become sullen, disagreeable, or withdraw from the family they see each day. In that cleavage that same young man is ready prey for the exciting illusion of some distant place.

What can the church do for the prodigal son? For one thing, the church can try to understand this clash without being shocked and upset. Perhaps the finest accomplishment of groups such as the Luther League is that they provide a setting where young people can discuss their common clashes with another generation in the atmosphere of understanding and sympathy. To do that, at the same time keeping contact with the Eternal, is to do what this young man of Jesus' story at his lowest ebb discovered was necessary. The memory of a home and the patient persistence of a waiting father pulled him back to usefulness.

These pressures for adventure, recognition, and something to satisfy the burning conflicts of his own soul are evident in every normal young person. Young people have a desire to know, a curiosity about what it is that makes some persons successful, how best to express themselves, how to meet new problems in developing leadership, and how to understand other groups and other religions. An intelligent, imaginative leader can be the difference between the headlong rush of youth to kick over the traces or an adequate stability for the years of pressure. At that point, he discovers the inner warmth, the quiet certainty of understanding which is the correlative of an abiding faith.

Recently a young family was caught in an auto accident in which the husband was killed, the wife horribly hurt. Through the months of coma and then the emergence through the bewildering experience of her new world, this young woman would cry out, "I do not believe." The pastor could only quietly say, "You don't have to believe now. Trust me. I will believe and you just trust." Something like that has to happen as we deal with those searching for a deepened faith. In the shock-experience of coming into an area of life which is new and somewhat frightening, they need the companionship of some who do believe, who have laid hold of large convictions, persons whom they can trust intellectually and spiritually. The first contribution of the church to the amateur adult is the gift of new friendship with personalities whose imagination and alert faith make them ready companions for young people who need a substitute parent.

Another problem illustrated by this parable is the difficulty confronted when a young person is in new surroundings where the old home ties are broken. The greatest mass migration of all history has occurred within the shores of our own country. Where in previous decades a family lived in one place for generations, families are now uprooted and moved within a few short months. With the old ties broken, the necessity of re-establishing friendships and the need for becoming something besides anonymous are problems familiar to every alert pastor.

In the shift from rural to urban populations and in the dispersal of industries, families are moved about with increasing frequency. The five moving firms constituting Allied Vans report moving at least three times as many families as before World War II; one firm is moving ten times as many. Allied Vans also reports that one out of seven of its customers will move again to a new state next year; seven out of ten will move again within five years. Such mobility necessarily creates a social problem.

Furthermore, the old group purpose of the family is disintegrated. New modes of transportation only serve to send the members of the family on larger forays for success. The cave man of other days went out as far as he could in search for food, returning to the safety of his little home by nightfall. In time he learned to team up with another fellow, build his fire, and remain overnight in a spot, searching for new and unspoiled hunting grounds. All the while he left his wife and children alone in the cave. That began the traveling salesman chapter of human society which has been accentuated by intercontinental travels which now bid fair to start men hungering for interstellar adventures. Even churches demand such longtime absences of their officials and their pastors that the family—and the church family—have found it necessary to think in totally new concepts of the life of the pastor.

The problem, difficult enough for the mature adult, is heightened for the young person. The necessity of making new friends and keeping something which can be a religious purpose is as difficult as it is for the prodigal son to find soul satisfaction near the pigsty. He knows that satisfaction of nerve-ends, sipping and tasting, is not the final answer. He wants something else. In Thornton Wilder's play "Our Town," the stage manager, as the commentator on what takes place in the play, introduces the concluding act with the statement: "I don't care what they say with their mouths—everybody knows that something is eternal. And it ain't houses, and it ain't names and it ain't earth and it ain't stars—everybody knows in their bones there is something eternal and that something has to do with human beings. All the greatest people that ever lived keep telling us that for five thousand years and yet you'd be surprised how people are always losing it. There's something down deep that's eternal about every human being." [2] If this is a feeling, the duty of the church is to give substance to that feeling.

Some of that will happen in the regular organizations of the church. That church which does not provide for that companionship of its young people, no matter how large a group or how small, has lost an opportunity of enormous significance. The alert and creative programs of such groups as the Luther League of America, distilled through the imaginative and understanding pastor or youth leader, can spell the difference between a youth settling down to live in the pigsty of life or the young person with the memory of home regardless of his present circumstances.

There is another personality in this story that needs our concern. He is the older brother at home, the fellow who didn't go away, but who stayed on grumbling at home. Somehow in our church work we seem to give official approbation to those who stay on even when they creatively add nothing to the scene. As a matter of fact, this elder brother was guilty of a worse heresy, namely that of a smug satisfaction with things as they are. He was opposed to any evangelism, any stewardship, any redemption and outreach of the kingdom. He not only enjoyed a broken family, he wanted to maintain the division. He liked the self-righteousness which he got into his own soul from just standing by. He was like Huckleberry Finn's aunt, and there are many of them in the church, "dismal, regular and decent." There is no glory about him at all. A part of our work with young people is in protecting ourselves from unwittingly canonizing these

[2] Thornton Wilder, *Our Town* (New York: Coward-McCann, 1938), p. 101.

dismal ones, giving young people a picture of righteousness in terms of the elder brother. We will frighten them off by this dull and solemn caricature of righteousness. The redemption of humanity is defeated by any effort to maintain the broken divisions of mankind.

In the crisis situation it was neither logic nor information that kept that young man from settling down by the pigsty, marrying a girl there, taking up residence at that place and rearing his children with only a distant nostalgic memory of home, told at infrequent times during a lifetime. Instead it was the memory of home, the remembrance of the meaning of life, a restoration of values, or, as the gospel tells it with magnificent economy of words, "He came to himself."

Victor Murray in his stimulating volume *Education Into Religion* emphasized in the contemporary scene the assertion of Dr. Reu in his generation concerning the importance of joining emotion and action. Emotions are sudden and momentary feelings—but when built into a sentiment, there is a pull to action. When there are no strong feelings, a young person striving for decision is cut adrift. One of the most important areas of our religious life will be at the point of the education of emotions, the development of larger loyalties, the growth of a sense of belonging. People are held in times of pressures not by logic nor by moralisms nor by the threats of disciplinary action. They are held by emotional ties. When the church, in its own life and in its thrust at strengthening the home, develops this calm in the storm, this certainty for persons cut adrift, this knowledge of something stable, it contributes that which the Ark did for the nomadic peoples of Israel. In all of their wanderings they still knew that there was one God and that they must guide their conduct by that fact.

The maturing process is a kind of walking along a boulevard of contraries. It is a walk that we think we take alone. As a matter of fact, when a man comes to himself it is as a result of a complex of factors. When the pressures are on the amateur adult as exemplified in this magnificent story told by Jesus, there must be an emotional pull, an inner courage and new design of the very shell of life, a redeeming of life itself, and a knowledge of concern beyond self.

"If I find in myself a desire which no experience in this world can satisfy, the most probable explanation is that I was made for another world. If none of my earthly pleasures satisfy it, that does not prove that the universe is a fraud. Probably earthly pleasures were never meant to satisfy it, but only to arouse it, to suggest the real thing." [2]

Thus, writes Luther, "The Holy Spirit teaches us the knowledge of Christ. He pours Him into the heart, setting it all on fire with love and making it steadfast through faith in Him, Where He dwells, there, please God, is fulness of life, whether the soul be weak or strong.

"And, that Christ dwells in our hearts means nothing else than to know who He is and what we may hope of Him, that is, that He is our Saviour through whom we have been brought into that state where we can call God our Father, and receive through Him the Spirit who gives us courage in the face of all calamities. Thus He has made our hearts His abode, and we cannot lay hold on Him in any other way, because He is not a dead thing, but the living God. But how can He be contained in the heart? Not by thoughts, but by living faith alone. He cannot be possessed through works, nor can looking draw him. Only the heart can hold Him. If, then, your faith is right and sound, you can both have and feel Christ in your heart, and know everything that He thinks and does in heaven and on earth, and how He rules through His Word and Spirit, and what is the mind of both those who possess Him and who do not possess Him." [3]

The second glimpse into the method of Jesus in dealing with

[2] C. S. Lewis, *Christian Behaviour* (New York: Macmillan, 1943), p. 57.
[3] Martin Luther in *Day by Day We Magnify Thee*, p. 230.

young persons under pressure is in the story of the rich young ruler, that possessor of the trinity of American virtues: wealth, youth and power.

This young man wanted no projects, no aptitude tests, no sermons, but he did want answers to his questions. He was the earnest seeker for a theological faith. He went away sorrowing chiefly because Jesus' answer not only went to the heart of his question, but likewise bridged from that answer to his personal life. Here was a man, much like Alsop's description of Oppenheimer as "the dangerous innocent," the person who while mentally alert could not see that there was a very definite relationship between what he believed and what he was, between what he thought out concerning his ultimate destiny and his present conduct. He is the young person who is aware of the fact that he must find answers to his questions and needs to understand the revolution that is occasioned by the discovery of the answer.

Nevin Harner lists six basic needs of all young people:

1. They need to find God
2. They must find themselves
3. They must find their life work
4. They must find their life mate
5. They must find their place in society and their relation to it
6. They must find their place in Christian society and their relation to it.[4]

The answer to these quests involves a strengthening of faith, a building of inner resources for the external pressures which society imposes upon us. Jesus' method of answering this young man is to place him into the full stress of responsibility. It is the method of reaching through his eternal quest to a personal situation.

[4] Nevin Harner, *Youth Work in the Church* (Nashville: Abingdon-Cokesbury, 1952), p. 31.

In a sense, "We love people in general but not in particular. And that's what most of our professional religious activity amounts to. Our church institutions and our professional ways of work are designed to manage and manipulate people in the abstract, but not to love them in the concrete. We traffic too much in dehumanized and despiritualized religion. The difficulty in dealing with God or man in the concrete is that you can't do it without having to deal with yourself. You can't get close to human brokenness without becoming conscious of your own brokenness or without having the sham of what you usually trust in, sorely revealed. From such intimate encounter comes a kind of humility which, if we had it would disabuse us of the confidence we have in so much doing good—so much preoccupation with institutional operation." [5]

Many is the person who is willing to talk with you about eternity but wants you to leave out of that discussion his own dealing with the present. Morality in the end is a very present problem. We need to answer those questions concerning eternal life and we need a theology of confrontation. That fact of the awesomeness of God that challenges a young person to handle the thing which stands between him and the fulfilment of his dearest desire is forever the need that the church recognizes.[6]

Frankly, our plans, our conferences, our organizations and our thinking of our young people has to be in the terms of these young men and women in our midst who are rich young rulers, men and women who possess more than young people have ever possessed. They have things, power, freedom, equipment and the energy to use all of this and they are troubled as to just where it is all getting them. If Christ is at the very center of life and history, if there is a living Word of God, if there is a truth that can be communicated, then it is to the specific needs of this present.

[5] Wm. N. Hawley, "Joey: a Sermonic Variation on an Ancient Parable," University of Chicago Divinity School *News*, August, 1954.
[6] Nevin Harner, *op. cit.*, p. 3.

"Man has been a dazzling success in the field of intellect and 'know-how' and a dismal failure in things of the spirit, and it has been the greatest tragedy of human life on earth that this sensational inequality of man's respective achievements and the spiritual sphere should at any rate have been this way round; for the spiritual side of man's life is the vastly greater importance for man's well-being (even for his material well-being in the last resort) than his command over non-human nature." [7]

The fact of eternal life has something to do with our relationship to our country, to ourselves, and to things. So Robinson Jeffers writes,

> How can we know, this is bad, this is good,
> When we know nothing about it, having no standards
>   * * *
> Nor faith to judge by? Like flies in a vacuum.
> Either we are animals—clever in some ways
> Degenerate in others, and follow instinct
> Or else we are something else and ought to do otherwise
>   * * *
> I wish to God I had some religion. [8]

That is what we confront. To teach that kind of religion and confront them with it, and match the collapse of a hedonistic culture with a religion that has stuff to it—to do this is to give amateur adults strength for the increasing pressures.

The third glimpse is in one incident in the life of the disciple John, the beloved—the faithful, who was standing there at the Cross, lost in sorrow at the crucifixion of his beloved Lord. Then the words, "Son, behold thy mother." There in that picture you have a brief glimpse at the lost sorrowing youth of our own time. There will be a fuller reference to this fact of lostness and sorrow in a later chapter, but it must be stated here as we explore some of the ways in which Jesus dealt with the pressures that

[7] Arnold Toynbee, *Civilization on Trial* (New York: Oxford, 1947), p. 262.
[8] Robinson Jeffers, *Be Angry at the Sun* (New York: Random House, 1941), pp. 14, 15, and 53.

are upon the amateur adult. Young people are amazingly sensitive to this lostness, this unrelatedness, this drifting about. Jesus' brief statements, committing a young man to a task, is one of those flashing glimpses of insight when it was never craftily done. It is the gasp of a dying man committing a young man to a task. There is vocation about it, and command. There is understanding about it. He took a sorrowing young adult and sent him, not lost in his grief, but committed to new responsibility. He does not dodge nor deny this tragedy; he transmutes it into a new relationship.

That was it. You have to do more than sympathize with young people in trouble. You have to startle them to new responsibilities. You have to commit them to new tasks. You have to call them out of their grief. In a sense they never look for sympathy. What they do need is this belongingness—this relatedness—this sense of a strengthening of faith for the pressure of loneliness.

You remember how the Scriptures state it: "we are surrounded by so great a company of witnesses, therefore let us run with patience the race that is set before us."

This is the ability to know the sorrow and yet to run the race, to understand the grief and yet to handle the problem, to be in the whole stream of life and thought, instead of stagnating in the backwash of pity and despair.

It is somehow to keep interpreting and reinterpreting the fact that Communion is the vehicle of grace to the inner man, relating the lonesome lost life to the suffering Christ, to the omnicompetence of God. When that has happened, we are well on our way to relating men and women to the present, delivering them out of despondency and depression to healthy relationships within the church or within society. There is no retreat to the old nostalgia. No matter how they wished it differently, Jesus was hanging on a cross. To implore John just to remember the old days wasn't going to transform him into a radiant personality. It is as new men, in new situations, that we can, by the mercies

of God, present our bodies as a living sacrifice, holy and acceptable, which is our reasonable service. This is the new relationship, the new structure and form of the community which
effectively disintegrates the selfish immorality of personal pity
and redeems us as of the household of God.

PROBLEM OF COMMUNICATION

Civilization's exacting problem in the midst of this era of pressure is communication, the challenge of announcing an idea which
can be interpreted in the midst of the conflicting tugs of modern
life. A few years ago, President Bevis of Ohio State University
stated that the achievement of the year on that campus was the
publishing of a lexicon whereby the professors of the various
colleges could speak with one another. The startling problem
of our time which requires the united action of diverse professions
makes it impossible for any man to be content to live with his
own professional or technical vocabulary.

This becomes particularly true of the problem confronting
young people. They have been taught words and concepts
which now must be stated in the midst of new pressures. They
must have the ability to discriminate. "The real problem of
'values' in mass communication is not how much volume—how
much sex—how much drinking—how many penthouses—how
many unpublished murders, but rather the nature of the operation
which produces a selectivity in such matters." If the religious
training they have received is alien from this new experience
they will be like the house described by Jesus, swept and
garnished and waiting for seven new devils.

Most of our young people coming from the experience of confirmation believe that there is a potential force and strength in
this faith into which they have been introduced. They need to
find it interpreted in their own experience. It is just at this place
where he is liable to find that his parents do not understand

his language and he feels a sense of clash between the generations. When a parent loses contact with growing young persons, and the church of which he is a part has lost contact, then he is unable to communicate with those allies who would stand with him at the most important and critical juncture of his experience.

He is conscious of the impulses which drive him hard—a push of instinctive energies in which he rejoices, yet which may be too much for him and land him in chaos. He needs a counter agent. "Sentiment," Dr. Yeaxlee calls it, "which exerts a pull is an attractive force. It works in the open. He realizes that though the influence upon him of objects which may become the centers of sentiments in one sense exerts itself independently of him, in another, he is free to choose or reject it. He can apply his powers of discrimination between values, and ally himself with the nobler." [9]

It is because of this that the church must constantly speak creatively and succinctly into the area in which young people live. At best, it will be difficult. But it must be a kind of speech which is aware that a maturing adult desires more than peace. "Of all things he hates the faulty faultless, icily regular, splendidly null. He wants to be the captain of his soul in order that he may throw himself into some quest or conquest. Unification of his resources is not enough. There must be a purpose. Nor may the purpose be narrow and ungenerous, concerned with nothing but his own welfare and position. He is waiting to give himself away in order that he may find himself." [10]

In a sense the task confronting us is that of giving counter-pressures to this young person caught in the world of pressures, pressures which can sustain him inwardly and give his creative growth, in fact, a growing faith.

[9] Basil A. Yeaxlee, *Religion and the Growing Mind* (Greenwich, Conn.: Seabury, 1952), p. 134.
[10] *Ibid.*, p. 131.

THE EMERGING TEMPTATIONS

A great many of us are good because we have not had a chance to go bad. My father had a maple tree which he planted on the front lawn of our home. There, propped up by guy wires, the little tree withstood the winter winds. When great oaks and elms fell in the storms, this little maple would stand, thanks to the propping wires. It is a symbol of many a person who unconsciously profits from the supports of family, church, and reputation.

Recently, two little thirteen-year-old boys, from respectable homes, decided that they needed more spending money than they were receiving. Because they had been reading of hold-ups, because they had seen robberies so frequently on television programs, because they were living now when they could more readily become responsive to influence of this sort they took a knife and tried to frighten the owner of a delicatessen store into giving them the contents of the cash register. Instead of being frightened, in this particular instance, the owner simply stood her ground and told the youngsters they ought to be ashamed of themselves.

A few years later, those same youngsters might have guns. Now the situation is changed because they have power in their hands. Place automobiles, arms and equipment into the hands of emotionally mixed up youngsters, and you have produced many of the situations which are the pressures upon the amateur adults. These are the young people who have biologically arrived at the place where they are no longer children but they have not achieved the maturity whereby they can handle the pressures which society places upon them.

When a church keeps alive the avenues of interest, affection and understanding, it is providing effective supports for the development of a personality of worth. This is preventive medicine, a kind of effective "guying up" of the personality through difficult and stormy years until the individual is mature enough to stand strong and humble enough to understand his constant need of the props of family, reputation and personality.

FOUR CONTRIBUTIONS TO BE MADE BY THE CHURCH

What contributions can the church make to those prodigals, these young rulers, these grieving Johns? Beyond the excellence of methods developed and resources available, let it be said once and for all that the finest contribution is in a church of excellence in preaching, excellence in pastoral ministry, excellence in personal concern. No pat method, no subtle lure, no concocted device will be an adequate substitute. Read the letters that come from servicemen; they all say the same thing. Their memories of the church at home are for them the thing most needful. Answers to a letter sent to many men in various parts of the world asking for suggestions from their vantage point for the program of the coming year said simply, "Do what you are doing. We want to remember the church active, alert, filled. Nothing gives us more of a sense of confidence and belonging as the knowledge that our church is there and at work."

The second contribution the church can make to these growing minds is the example of a deepened faith. We let young people off and down by our example of faithlessness. They want to see people who have conquered doubts and handled problems. Paul was forever telling people "Mark me as an example." God knows that we clergymen falter when it comes to saying that, and our laymen forget it as well.

Here is a churchman who expressed his distaste for newcomers to our country and for any solution of the problems of racial understanding. He said of a recent sermon of his pastor, "I expect you to believe this, but don't expect me to believe it. I'm only a layman." That attitude of cynicism poisons the minds of young people. Say they, and with good reason, "We should like to see the example of these people. Didn't Jesus say, 'By their fruits you shall know them'?" The finest contribution the church can make to the strengthening of faith is the creation of the fellowship of young people with men and women of a great faith, men and women who exemplify their spirit of courage, of resolution, of the vitality to cope with the mountainous problem of our time with a measure of hopefulness and strength.

The third contribution we can make is that of empathy. One of the difficulties in the personality of Paul was just at this point. His discouragement with homesick Mark sent Mark to Cyprus. It was Barnabas who was the minister of encouragement, who for seventeen years worked with this young man until Paul could call for Mark to come to him in his last moments. What would have come to Mark's ministry had it not been for Barnabas? Sometimes the church in its sense of the greatness of the task becomes "Pauline" in this oversight or lack of understanding of the homesickness of its young people. Because of one exploit, or one fall along the way, or one example of faithlessness, we are willing to cast them off. The church that ministers to young people today will be one which will understand the depths of their character and will assist to educate the emotional pull toward a deepened and abiding faith. Faith doesn't come in a moment. It is the result of growth, of the long pull toward truth and righteousness.

The fourth contribution is in the extra-curricular, or personal discussions of faith. In the earlier churches men and women were schooled in the Christian cause in private sessions with their pastor. Our overworked schedules and busied days make this well-nigh impossible. And yet, increasingly it must occur. Most of us will testify to the happiness that has come when a few young people, gathered at the fireplace or in the study, have gotten down to bedrock and talked about the problems which beset them and their need of a growing faith. It will never be done in large groups or in assemblages. They help, but in the end, it will be in the schooling in personal ways and in the challenge of mind and thought in personal conference.

On a recent journey from Philadelphia to Buffalo, I met a hard-bitten businessman at breakfast in the diner, and we conversed concerning many of the day's happenings. He did not know my profession and spiced his discussion with "purple language." Soon, into the diner came a family of a mother and father and ten children. They were obviously immigrants from another country, and instantly the talk of all of us was concerning this family. We listened to their conversation trying to ascertain their nationality. My friend indicated that we had too many foreigners in this country and it was time somebody did something about it.

One of the family spoke some English and so gave the order for the meal. In due time the waiters arrived with twelve plates of eggs and bacon and we watched the little children eagerly begin to eat. At long last, the parents were served. Whereupon the father rapped on the table with his fork and everyone stopped eating, hands were folded, heads were bowed and in good strident Dutch, the father began to pray. At his "Amen" the family joined in a group prayer.

When the prayer was completed, my friend wiped a tear from his eye and with almost liturgical reverence said, "Damn it all, God bless them." He was with me to shepherd them from one station to another when we arrived in Buffalo. He lamented loudly that they were going on to Canada—that we ought to have such persons in America.

I wonder about them. Now they have an inherited tradition, a vital piety, a kind of witnessing faith. When they have become acclimated, when the years have gone by, will they still pray? Will they still have a sense of family unity? Will they still be aware of God's guiding care? What will the pressures of the years do to these persons as they mature and come to their independence in their new country? In a sense, they become the symbols of the situation confronted by every young person. Either we shall help them in church and home to have the sympathetic understanding, the nostalgic memories of gladness, the understanding of a basic unity and the foundation for a maturing faith, or we shall have missed one of our most challenging moments. To be strengthened in faith is to have the inner courage to be in the world and yet not of it, to be unafraid and able to say "Here I stand, I can do no other."

SOME SUGGESTIONS FROM OTHERS

One pastor surveyed his congregation, inquiring concerning their problems and besetting worries. He repeated that in many instances they shared the same general problems. Out of his survey he has mapped a continuing "sharing-between-the-generations" panel program which is assisting varying age groups to meet present-day pressures with Christian knowledge.

Another church reports that the greatest need felt in that parish was for a rethinking of the essentials of faith, not as discussion of ethics or of current problems. This pastor believes that Luther's genius in translating into the language of his day needs to be emulated by a kind of translation into today's area of thinking of the essential articles of faith. The average pastor will say, "But that's what I thought I was doing." Perhaps we have, but then college young people and young married couples wistfully say to us, "We need to rethink our faith in order to stand up against today's pressures."

Book reviews of volumes such as Hordern's *Layman's Guide to Protestant Theology* (Macmillan, 1955), whet the appetite for the building of an inner faith to withstand pressures. Pastors report that they have gotten further with such continuing adventures than with classes. There is a new urgency for the retreat type of meeting, the area where pastor and young people can find the time to read Scripture, pray, think in current terms and meet problems honestly. It's a breaking down of the cleavages or professional isolationism which can creep in.

III

Yearning for Vocation

To Thy Growth in Grace

+

All too many people are doing things which they do not want
to do. They feel that they have no way out of their squirrel
cage. They are troubled as were the crowds in Jesus' day, as
Luke records. They would like to reach out and touch him with
their hands, "for power was going from him and he was healing
them all." Yet they are not sure that this is the power they
need. A clinical analysis of those who have come to middle life
and have taken anything of a long look at their careers will
reveal that a goodly percentage look back with regret that time
has slipped and so little has been done. Most counselors find
themselves dealing with unhappy people who remark, "When
I was young, I thought I would be a doctor, or a minister, or a
lawyer, or a woodworker, or a farmer," and then they drift off
with the long stories of the factors which thwarted their decisions. In short, they have lost the sense of vocation.

It is one thing to minister to those who have regrets. It is
another to deal with those with dreams. This is one of the major
opportunities of the church. For in a generation when almost
every school or group has leaders in occupational guidance, few
have leaders in vocational guidance. The church can create
constructive habits in mental and spiritual health.

It is in the church that men discover that they are not alone in the struggle. The loneliness of a man's adventure in life is never more poignant than in the industrialized settings of today. Flattened by catastrophic events, dwarfed by enormous international problems and trapped by circumstances which cannot be changed, man loses contact with God, with his neighbor, and with his own self. The church at its best will be the society of those who have discovered that they can be in league with those who have the power to become the sons of God.

This power, which the Gospels describe as the grace of God, is referred to constantly by Paul as that cohesive power which holds together both a man within himself and the community into which he is set. To place the words of Jesus concerning seeking the kingdom, first into the modern setting of people rushing madly for worldly goods is Christianity's special challenge in this generation. "So don't worry and don't keep saying, what shall we eat and what shall we drink, or what shall we wear. Your heavenly Father knows that you need them all— Set your heart on his kingdom and his goodness and all these things will come to you as a matter of course." [1]

It is in this recognition of the practical business of living and the need for power beyond oneself that vocational guidance is given at its best. To grow in grace is to mature in the knowledge of vocation. We are called and so we serve. The gift of the Christian doctrine of grace is in the fact that a man is not a solitary struggler for either his daily bread or his own welfare. He belongs to that family of God. The lonesomeness of the struggle for life is broken through by the enormity of God's concern. Once we have accepted the fact of God's existence, we have come to the next step, that of the recognition of God's concern. That concern is known best in the fact of the incarnation and appreciated best in the fact of the atonement. Luther's

[1] See Matthew 6:25-33.

insistence that these two doctrines be kept in the same sentence produces his similar concern that the ancient lines between secular and sacred be abolished. God's gift to life and his sacrifice for life sanctify the whole of life. God calls. Man yearns to know that call. In that fact and in its acceptance or denial hangs the balance in the struggle for ethical integrity, the right of the worker for his hire, and the yearning for some reason for it all.

"When they had finished breakfast, Jesus said to Simon Peter, 'Simon, son of John, do you love me more than these?' He said to him, 'Yes, Lord; you know that I love you.' He said to him, 'Feed my lambs.' A second time he said to him, 'Simon, son of John, do you love me?' He said to him, 'Yes, Lord; you know that I love you.' He said to him, 'Tend my sheep.' He said to him the third time, 'Simon, son of John, do you love me?' Peter was grieved because he said to him the third time, 'Do you love me?' And he said to him, 'Lord, you know everything; you know that I love you.' Jesus said to him, 'Feed my sheep.' " [2]

So Jesus dealt with his closest friends and so he deals with us. It was a baffling series of questions to this man who felt he had given everything to this high adventure. To Jesus it was not at all baffling. It was the building up of a purpose that would hold this stormy character through all manner of temptation until he stood strong and unshakable at Pentecost.

The greatest fact in the Christian way of life is that God is.

The greatest faith in the Christian way of life is that God cares.

The greatest hope in the Christian way of life is that God is redeeming mankind.

That makes each of us a part of this kingdom. Certainly Peter loved his Lord, but he needed to be a full part of it all. "You see, Peter, I've made you a part of this. You're no longer just

[2] John 21:15-16 (R.S.V.).

an admirer of mine. It isn't just that all of this love you feel is something directed to you, there to take up residence forever. You're a person, Peter. All of this love will be tested. You've built for a cause. If you keep all of this love for yourself, all of this building-up in you will come to a place of breakdown. Take your love and share it, risk it, adventure with it. Feed sheep and lambs. Teach people, win lives, share your all. The gates of new life are thrown open to you. He that loses his life shall find it." It's as though he spoke to Peter like that.

When the North American Lay Conference on "The Christian and His Daily Work" met in Buffalo in February, 1952, it concerned itself with this challenge, "We and our churches must show more concern for what happens between Sundays. We must change the attitude that makes Christian living into Sunday living. In other words, we must banish the ignorance and indifference toward what is going on in the so called lay-world between Sundays. God is no respecter of persons nor of occupations so long as the work involved is useful work, and from the Protestant view the church is represented by its laity just as much as by it clergy. In fact more so because there are so many more of us laymen, each his own high priest before God. We are not to discuss the relation of Christianity in general terms but very specifically in that part of life where the individual Christian earns his daily living. The challenge of the governments of the world today is how to make man both economically secure and free. The challenge to Christians under those governments is how to live the whole gospel the whole week, all seven days."

At Evanston in 1954 this challenge was repeated when men expressed the desire to discover a sense of integrity for their work, relationship with their brothers, and a knowledge of some power for the handling of the daily challenges of life.

We are called, gathered and enlightened to be godly. No one, aware of the saving grace of God's love, will ignore this knowledge of being in league with God's power.

THE FORMATIVE YEARS AND VOCATION

Young people confront a period of maturing wherein the difficulties of emancipation from the old ties initiate numerous conflicts. Young people have to decide somewhere along the way what they are to do with their lives, where they are going to spend their careers, with whom they are going to live and just what they want most out of life. Parents and counselors are aware of these facts and in most instances honestly want to help. Wise counselors know that they cannot take over. Many of the storms of adolescence begin when eager parents attempt to control the choices of young people. Because there are parents who are afraid to emancipate their children or to understand with any patience or faith the stormy periods of "growing up," there are constant conflicts.

Every pastor knows the parent who says, "My daughter has never been away from me, and I have never been away from her for all of these years." The other extreme is the parent who is busy with his own affairs and so unconcerned with what is happening to the child that he is unaware of the schedules, the desires, the hopes of the young person. No more significant contribution to the health of a nation is made than in the creation of homes where this belonging to God's care and concern is translated into an intelligent awareness of continuity in the life of young persons. Somehow we shall have to more creatively guide young people in the growth of an awareness of God's grace in order that they can make free, independent, and responsible choices which lead to profession, to marriage, and to the development of the habits which determine so much of their future.

In recent surveys of pastor and parents in varying kinds of churches this has been done by parent-child conferences or group discussions, where both parents and young people have an opportunity to speak. One church reported success in assisting this selection of vocation by career days, calling in persons within the church for conference periods with young people. For instance, in a number of cities, symphony orchestras have periods within the season when aspiring young violinists, cellists, trumpeters are given an opportunity to sit next to the professional musician, and play in a special concert under the direction of the conductor. Our young people go into the city hall and spend a day in the various civil offices. Or they go into the newspaper offices or hospitals to learn of the procedures in these institutions. All of these successful endeavors are possible for a select few. What can happen is a similar experiment within the church. There are imaginative pastors who are bringing varying professions and young people together for conferences on the life of a Christian in business, in law, in medicine, in any number of varying jobs and professions. When a man has a chance to sit down to speak out concerning the problems of his own job, he himself can feel a new sense of dignity and responsibility about it. By the same token, the young person has had an opportunity to discuss the matter first hand.

It is one thing for a man to be talking about his vocation in one of the professions. It is quite another matter when he is a worker on an assembly-line or a laborer in one of the enormous industries. This discussion of vocation has to do with the wholeness of life. One of the most successful discussions this writer has ever witnessed was when men who work in automobile factories actually sat down to discuss the problems of their jobs, the relationship with the unions, the aspirations, hopes and difficulties of their jobs and of the significance of their Christian faith in relation to their jobs. We are forever pressed back to the fact that when the Christian speaks of vocation he speaks of his calling to be a man of God. He is not talking about success financially or socially or professionally. He is talking of being the best that he knows from this knowledge of self and of God's concern for him. It is this security we want to give the young people of this generation.

PLACING A PERSON IN COMMUNITY

As has been pointed out in the previous chapter, one of the most useful gifts of a church to its young people is a sense of belonging or community. That relationship to young people of similar age groupings such as the Luther League, the Lutheran Student Association, and other such groups is of invaluable significance. Young people who discover relationships of emotional significance in such societies find an inner satisfaction which ties into their daily work. Just as the personnel bureau of an alert industry is concerned that the home life of its employees be happy because unhappiness or happiness will affect the quality and efficiency of the work accomplished, just so the social relationships of a young person affect both his educational career and his personality development. The fact that young people in Sunday school and youth groups are not involved in crime and delinquency is not due to any kind of magic; it is the simple fact that they have found a satisfaction for their emotional needs in a wholesome environment and had found some satisfactory releases for their need to belong.

SIX STEPS IN BELONGING

1. *God's Grace Empowers*

The grace of God needs to have emotional significance for growing young people even as it has theological significance for the whole Christian faith. "Even when I was a little child I was conscious that I was I because of him," said Eleanor Wilson McAdoo looking at her distinguished father. This sense of belonging, this sense of relationship, of God coming to man, is one of the finest gifts of a healthy home to growing young people and is matched in the theological sense by this understanding of a universe in which man is more than a lonely struggler.

> O Lord, thou hast searched me and known me!
> Thou knowest when I sit down and when I rise up;
> Thou discernest my thoughts from afar . . .

Thou dost beset me behind and before,
    and layest thy hand upon me . . .
Whither shall I go from thy Spirit?
    Or whither shall I flee from thy presence?
If I ascend to heaven, thou art there!
    If I make my bed in Sheol, thou art there!
If I take the wings of the morning
    and dwell in the uttermost parts of the sea,
even there thy hand shall lead me,
    and thy right hand shall hold me . . .
Search me, O God, and know my heart!
    Try me and know my thoughts!
And see if there be any wicked way in me,
    and lead me in the way everlasting! [3]

This is the confession of faith made by one who has discovered for himself that the power of God is no distant academic fact but a reality.

When we help young people to understand this fact, we have helped them to travel the long road from the heritage of doctrines to a personal religious experience.

2. *Christianity Is Concerned with Wholes*

Surprising to most young persons is the sudden awareness that their religious experience has something to do with the whole of life. They have thought of religion in terms of general behavior. It was a matter of not stealing, or committing murder. So it had to do with coming to church. But it is something of a first-rate religious experience, which even many adults have not had, more's the pity, to realize that one's faith has something to do with the whole of one's being.

It is the sudden consciousness that success in life is due to more than education, skill, and good fortune in making the right contacts. It has to do with the whole person. This, which seems elemental to the pastor, is radical to many an individual. It may

[3] Psalm 139 (R.S.V.).

even be radical in the thinking of the church in relationship to its people and its environmental setting.

So, as Henry P. Van Dusen says, "Religion yields wisdom not by adding to our information but by furnishing a perspective where that information may be truly seen, and then by supplying norms through which that information may be rightly appraised, by sensitizing and training our latent intuitive sense for the value of facts and the meaning of events. All supremely important truth is truth of value. Not least economic, social and political truths, affecting as they do the intimate destinies of mankind's millions." [4]

Our whole is affected by our economic environment, or our social environment. It is also affected by our religious environment. When a church leads wisely, encouraging this wholeness of faith in its young people, it saves them from the shoddy promises of those who promise happiness by simply thinking it so, and salvation by crawling under the tables of big organizations. Freedom requires men of sturdy character, with a willingness to think religiously in "wholes." This is a part of growing grace.

3. *Christianity Relates Persons with Persons*

The Christ who hung from a cross took a grief-stricken woman and a grief-stricken young man, individuals utterly lost in their personal grief, and sent them away with new relationships. Christianity at its best is always doing that. It takes persons in the settings of their lives and relates them to one another. This is never more important than in the area of vocation. If we are to give young men and women a sense of belonging, of a call to be not only their best, but God's best for their lives, it will be achieved by relating them to persons who have attained spiritual maturity. They need to know someone, through per-

[4] H. P. Van Dusen, *God in These Times* (New York: Scribners, 1935), p. 137.

sonal experience or biography, who can be what Barnabas was to John Mark, the minister of encouragement.

Many young people's meetings have been blessed by having a dedicated physician talk about his work, an aviator share information concerning his profession, a labor union leader discuss the problems confronting workers. This is possible in cities or in small communities. Where individuals are not readily available there are always men or women who can use available literature to think with young people.

Beyond all of the techniques and the plans, which are all valuable, there is nothing that can take the place of the example of an all-round person. One person, with a hunger for life, a zest for all things, and creative imagination, can be of more significance than all of the novelties.

More than all of this, young people are persons. They want to belong. When they are related to godliness through personality, they belong. They are saved from the escapism of gangs, lured by creative imagination, belonging to the community of the righteous.

4. *Recognizing Values in Actual Work*

One of the encouraging trends of modern stewardship practice has been the discouragement of support for the church through money-making devices. The recognition of the loss of religious value and individual energy in such enterprises was overdue. The Lutheran Laymen's Movement for Stewardship and its leaders have been of incomparable value to the church in stressing once and for all the meaning of stewardship.

What is needed now is more than a kind of pharasaical happiness in what we don't do. To be done with bazaars and money-making is one thing; to have captured the time and imagination of people for other tasks is another thing. We have been too readily satisfied to have abolished a bazaar with nothing constructive to take its place. The state of that church is liable to be readied for the entrance of seven worse devils of sinister concern unless something else has filled this vacuum.

5. *Vocation Is Not a Calling to a Particular Occupation*

The church which insists on one hand that the ministry is the holiest of callings and then portrays a ministry which is neither vital nor powerful defeats itself. The holiness of the ministry as an occupation, a calling, needs no defense here. No man who has faced the challenges of a ministry in this modern world can fail to be staggered by its complexity and enormity. We fail the ministry unless we express in what we are the boldness of its power and the imagination it creates. But does God call men only to the ministry?

That ought hardly be asked of a Protestant group, thanks to our heritage. However, we are still bound too frequently by the pious assertion that giving oneself to God's call is to give oneself to the ministry. We need ministers, strong, alert, conscientious, intelligent ministers willing to adventure. All of this discussion of raising the salaries of ministers is important. What also needs to be raised is a sense of independence of thought and action and a trust in what a man can yet do, empowered by God.

Beyond this is the sense—the greater sense—of vocation as God's call to any man. We are called to be God's people and we need to express that in practical ways.

The calling grace of God places a man where he sees life and his relationship to it. God calls us to do God's will. From that vantage point a man chooses his profession.

This is the sense of vocation by which grace entered the mind and life of Albert Schweitzer. "I wanted to be a doctor" he writes, "that I might be able to work without having to talk. For years I had been giving myself out in words . . . this new form of activity I could not represent to myself as talking about the religion of love, but only as an actual putting it into practice. . . .

"Only at quite rare moments have I felt really glad to be alive. I could not but feel with a sympathy full of regret all the pain that I saw around me, not only that of men but that of the whole creation. "From this community of suffering I have never tried to withdraw myself. It seemed to me a matter of course that we should all take our share of the burden of pain which lies upon the world.

"People say I understand something about music, but the sweetest sound I have ever heard came from a room one night when from the change in a baby's crying I knew that the crisis had passed, and that he would be well again.

"[Christ] speaks to us the same word: 'Follow thou me!' and sets us to the tasks which He has to fulfil for our time. He commands. And to those who obey Him, whether they be wise or simple, He will reveal Himself in the toils, the conflicts, the sufferings which they shall pass through in His fellowship, and, as an ineffable mystery, they shall learn in their own experience Who He is." [5]

Here is grace become belonging, matured into fulfilment and come to vocation. It is the call not to a particular profession, but to the godliness of God, the holiness of belonging, the dedication of commitment. After confirmation, this is the venture which ought to beset every Christian young person and this is the challenge which confronts us as we lead people from an academic acceptance of a doctrinal truth to a personal acceptance of a doctrinal fulfilment.

6. We Are Channels of God's Grace

No more important factor can be demonstrated to growing minds than this simple statement of Christian truth. In a recent volume on pastoral preaching, David MacLennan urged: "A

[5] Albert Schweitzer, quoted in excerpts from Eugene Exman, *The World of Albert Schweitzer* (New York: Harper, 1955), in *Saturday Review*, January 15, 1955, pp. 13-14.

discipline all of us must undertake continuously is this: we must strive to communicate simply and vividly. Technical jargon, omnibus phrases which glitter but do not illumine, verbal abstractions dearly loved by intellectuals—these may impress; but they do not edify. Tell me the story simply, may be a juvenile request to make of professional scholars; it is a plea to the preacher by lay folks which must be heeded." [6]

The simple truth that needs to be stated in the approach to a sense of vocation is the glowing, vivid fact that we are all the channels of power. Religion was once defined as what a man does with his solitariness. True. But, it is also then what is done with all that he is in relation to his fellows. That church is strengthened wherein laymen assume the responsibilities of sharing truth, engaging in activities of religious significance that add strengh and sustaining meaning to their own jobs or professions.

At the point of actual vocation, many churches have kept in contact with their growing young people through participation in the liturgy of the church or the ceremonies. Guilds for young men who serve at the altar and who prepare the church for its worship services have been universally successful. A Timothy Club in my own church keeps me in contact with young people who have a sense of responsibility and orderliness, a sense of a call to the work of the church. This is a place where they can serve, where they can discuss the mores of their parents and others who attend church, where they can observe from every responsible point of view the whole aspect of worship.

Yet there is a danger. "The tendency on the part of young people to resort to rituals to avoid the feelings of guilt about the modes of expression of their inner impulses should be seriously considered by religious educators. Many children of this day try to form religion not because they understand or wish to lead better ethical and spiritual lives, but because the rituals and

[6] David A. MacLennan, *Pastoral Preaching* (Philadelphia: Westminster, 1955).

ceremonials of religion offer them temporarily an easier way of controlling the modes of expression of their inner impulses than having to learn how to deal with them from an ethical or sociological aspect. A child in the latent period is obverted. Having made his peace with his sense of guilt by placing all responsibility for his actions on the religious rituals and ceremonials—not on religion—he can then behave as he likes without feeling any guilt about his behavior. He can continue to behave as he likes as long as he performs the necessary rituals and prayers." [7]

This does not mean we should discard such liturgies. They are too important for that. It is necessary to recognize that we do have a problem in developing the sense of vocation, that we tie young people into the life of the church through these means. We ought not to stop there. If we did we would leave them with an understanding and even an appreciation of a mechanic of the church without developing any effective religious integrity. They are not going to remain at that church. They are not going to be always at that place. In military service, in distant places, under the pressure of the many problems of their lives, they will need more than participation in formal service. To fill that need, the contact with minister, with the congregation and with the worship services of the church will have to produce a calling to godliness, if it is to make its finest witness.

7. The Development of Significant Areas for Specialized Religious Vocation

One of the challenges confronting every program of evangelism is in the need for assimilation of dedicated talent and ability into the life of the church. All too many times men and women are galvanized by a religious rededication only to be told

[7] Oliver S. English and G. H. J. Pearson, *Emotional Problems of Living* (New York: Norton, 1945), p. 243.

that there is no task awaiting them comparable to the experience
and talent of the individual or the white heat of religious conviction. A layman, called to Christ, ought to be challenged to
do more than usher or count money, important as these tasks
are. We shall have to consider the possibilities of Christian leadership in terms of the seriousness with which the early church
confronted this responsibility.

The early disciples sought out seven men of good report and
laid upon them the heavy tasks of charity, of caring for the
needy, of witnessing. Among that company was Stephen, the
first Christian martyr. The church to these men was no hierarchy,
no mere stultified body. It was an organism, a living dynamic
action in the world. The Spirit of God moved through men,
and the persons to whom Paul wrote, to whom James gave
leadership, to whom Peter ministered, to whom Thomas witnessed were the men and women of the church. They were
doing the godliest of tasks, that of discharging their responsibilities of having been called into the holy fellowship of Christ
himself. "You are no more strangers and foreigners."

In the confused situation of our own time, while there is yet
a margin of possibility, the church must be about the task of
training all its men and women for tasks which challenge their
whole selves. It is not enough for them to do these few tasks
under the direction of a pastor. They are to be witnesses, free
men, they are to be marching under the leadership of a Christ
who has called, gathered, enlightened, and sanctified them. This
sense of leadership becomes the mightiest kind of challenge to
youth in the church. Here is our finest opportunity to train, to
lead, to guide, and to win men to the vocation of witnessing, men
who understand the need to grow in grace.

To use but one illustration, the whole area of lay witnessing
is vastly underrated and overlooked within the church. All over
our country in the burgeoning suburbs and new housing areas,
in the territories where the church is working in temporary

quarters, there is a need for trained personnel. In the days of Muhlenberg, men and women were trained to be lay leaders. In many a city today congregations in emergency situations call upon men—bankers, radio announcers, teachers—who have a superb faith and magnificent courage to lead pastorless churches. There are instances where, for as long as a year, a lay leader has maintained a congregation and given it magnificent witness. Yet in these instances no one has helped these men to grow in grace, or led them to a maturing knowledge of God's saving truth which they are to witness. They need now to have the friendship of a pastor, someone with whom they can meet from week to week, to read theology, to study the Word of God, to understand the principles of witnessing.

When we have done this we shall have given status to one of the neglected areas of the church's life. Our tragedy too frequently is that we have seen the dimensions of the gospel in the terms of the provincial boundaries of our own experience. When the Spirit moves within the human being there are new dimensions. This is what confronts the youth of our time. The crude men of our time have proven this. They have marshaled young men and women, charged them with responsibilities, read their unholy orders to them, and captured not only their minds but their ambitions and have sent them marching to do their bidding. In that situation the church has no business to be on the defensive. Through the ages the church has proclaimed its faith in the Holy Spirit, in the high calling of the gospel, in the growth of grace within the human being. It is at this aggressive imaginative focal point that the most daring work can be done with young people. They do not want a withdrawal into the cloisters. They do not want protection. They do not want to be set to tasks which are completely dimensioned by tradition. The church has had to learn how to behave in the underground, to retreat to the catacombs, to live in the time of tyranny. Now it has to live in the white light of publicity, in the time of communication, when men must articulate their faith and make their gospel known.

There is a legend from the Middle Ages which illustrates this honest desire. It is the story of the juggler who became a monk and tried in various ways of piety to find the peace that passeth understanding. Yet he was unhappy and knew that for all of his vows he had not found peace. Then one day he resorted to the thing he knew best. He went before the statue of the Virgin with his tricks of juggling. The scandalized abbot watched horrified at this undignified behavior and would have stopped it all. But the statue came to life, descended from its pedestal and graciously thanked the juggler for his sincere devotion, for the use of his finest talents.

We shall have to understand a man's talents and make the dimensions of the congregational life large enough to receive these varied abilities and use them. For the Christian faith is not a human contrivance. It is a calling to holiness, where grace grows until, strengthened in the full armor of God, a man witnesses. "There is an old spiritual, which Tin Pan Alley may have borrowed without so much as a by-your-leave" writes David MacLennan, "which has a recurring refrain, 'Rise, shine, give God glory.' That is it. Paul meant precisely that when he said, 'Therefore whether ye eat or drink or whatsoever ye do, do all to the glory of God.' The commonplace details of life can be, are lifted up as participants in the splendid enterprise God inaugurated and glorified." [8]

VOCATION IN THE FAMILY

Perhaps our most practical leadership must be given in preparing young people for a sense of call in the home. Both in the home in which they reside and the home in which they hope to find their ultimate happiness there must be the sense of calling.

[8] David MacLennan, *Joyous Adventure* (New York: Harper, 1952), p. 154.

Men and women are asked to withstand too many temptations, too many disturbances in life's situations, to wander into family relationships without a sense of God's moving grace. Yet early marriages and the desire to rush to experience life's fullest calling finds many persons spiritually unprepared.

Recently a group of forty young persons were discussing the many experiences which they had had in military service and in college. Over and over again there was a recurring refrain, "When I get home for good, I will do so and such." They meant to be home permanently. Yet what is a home for good, unless it is a home which is a laboratory, a clinic, a place of community, a place of reverence and faith? It is to be a home which grows in grace.

It is only a short distance from confirmation to marriage and young people seem to be breaking the distance record every day. Along with this, in America in the last 10 years 8 million persons were divorced. That means about 800,000 last year, leaving 300,000 children in broken homes. Preaching is not going to cure this situation. Leadership in the Christian way of life, preparing young people for marriage, for the building of a home, for the creation of healthy mental habits, for the giving of their fullest in mind and body to the grace of God, will result in happy grace-filled homes.

Whether they will or not, these young people must establish homes under the most diverse of circumstances. It was said of Abraham Lincoln, "he was the lord of his event." Never was there a more urgent time when a young person was asked to have the spiritual resources to be able to be the lord of the circumstances which beset him. They need counseling clinics, friendship with pastors who are understanding of the needs of life, the creation of a climate wherein pastors, parents, young people can discuss the problems of life, freely and frankly entering into the business of "growing grace."

When the Titanic struck the iceberg in the night and a shudder ran through the ship, there was no time to call the crew and give them a lecture on the manner in which they ought to behave. There was only time for the captain to call his crew together and say, "Be British." And they were. The men acquitted themselves as the traditions of the seas had dictated through the centuries. It is something of that kind of discipline and understanding that needs instinctively to be a part of our training and life.

Christ walked in the environment of much religiosity and came into full conflict with it. He insisted on a spirit that defied legalisms and was done with the petty. "These institutions were full of men who did all of the correct things, said all of the correct words, and doubtless were spiritual in many cases but gave off nothing that penetrated the imagination of others and made them want the same faith these people held. The non-conductors of the church receive and do not give out. They are terminals not junctions. Some of them are spiritual people with deep convictions. But one can hold convictions without knowing how to spread them persuasively. A great many people in the churches have convictions but not power. They have strong moral or theological beliefs but they are not contagious. Many clergy conduct the church's business but not the church's power. They have not learned to be natural or unself-conscious about their religion as if all the while they were in the midst of a great and fascinating experience and would love to include others in it." [9] These interesting observations of Dr. Samuel Shoemaker can be made of any denomination. They are not so much an indictment as they are an evidence of a deep and burning desire to have the sense of call, to grow in grace.

In all of the current search for happiness, for integrated personalities, and for peace of mind, the deepest yearning is for vocation. To know that you are doing what you are equipped and called to do, and to have a deep and abiding satisfaction

[9] Samuel Shoemaker, *op. cit.*, p. 92.

in it, is the goal of every mature person. The only difference between the generations is that today's young people have more opportunities to do something about it. The church at the critical moment dare not let its young people off and down. Many people are disappointed within the church. They have come searching for a challenge and they have no way to channel this new interest nor does the church seem to have anything to offer them. They want to grow as Christians and they want power to share truth. The eager way in which many people have run after all manner of will-o-the-wisps is a significant symptom of their eagerness to share. The danger with much of it is in the aftermath or hangover of disillusionment.

Gordon W. Allport has given us an almost classic definition of religion. "A man's religion," he says, "is the audacious bid he makes to bind himself to creation and to the Creator. It is his ultimate attempt to enlarge and to complete his own personality by finding the supreme contact in which he rightly belongs." [10] Here is vocation, the knowledge that one is called to belong, to become and so find a destiny. Men find this or they find a substitute. That is why false faiths can command such allegiance. These faiths, as Dr. Van Dusen writes, do not invite participation, they command allegiance; they do not persuade by hypothesis, they declare finalities; they do not promise satisfactions; they demand sacrifices; they do not pamper men, they conscript their souls.

Some are called to serve in this present age. Paul called on us to make it our vocation to present our bodies as a living sacrifice, challenging us to serve in respective ways with the creative imagination and with the patience of faith to run our race.

"Christians are called out of the world to be members of the new kingdom of grace and to participate in the new being that entered into the world to serve God there and to bring about

[10] Gordon W. Allport, *The Individual and His Religion* (New York: Macmillan, 1950), p. 142.

the transfiguration of the world according to his purpose.

"In so far as Christians refuse to accept this obligation and withdraw from participation in the activities of secular society, they have by an act of abdication handed over society to the direction of those who are non-Christians. They have declined responsibility in the combat against the powers of evil for the effective fulfilment of the Christian task in the world. It is right and necessary that some Christians should withdraw from secular pursuits to devote themselves as ministers of the gospel, wholly to the service of the new order manifested in Christ, and that these should be religious communities devoted toward working out intensively the deeper implications of the Christian faith and love. But such withdrawals have their end and meaning in relation to the warfare against evil which is waged in the actual life of the world. Their purpose is to bring support to those who are fighting in the front lines of the battle." [11]

The Christian knows that he is a citizen of two worlds and he believes that he is meant to live in this world as a child of God. It is at that point that he parts company from every attempt to enslave the person by the authoritarian, the big organization, the Marxist—all efforts driving men under the cover of some illusory promise or protection lead to the degradation of the human being. It is when a man is able to be a responsibly free, creatively useful person that he has the sense of vocation.

When Dietrich Bonhoeffer was caught in the maelstrom of the events of Hitler's Germany, he had to confront this sense of vocation. "The man who felt all the force of the pacifist position and weighed the cost of discipleship concluded in the depths of his soul that to withdraw from those participating in the political and military resistance would be irresponsible cowardice and flight from reality. Not, as his friend Bethge writes, that he believed that everybody must act as he did, but from where

[11] Joseph H. Oldham, *Life Is Commitment* (New York: Harper, 1952), p. 98.

he was standing he could see no possibility of retreat into any sinless, righteous, pious refuge. The sin of respectable people reveals itself in flight from responsibility. He saw that sin falling upon him and he took his stand." [12]

When we give a young person a call to become, to express himself in the various activities of the congregation and to recognize him as a person in the community of the church, we are assisting that young man to become a healthy personality, a person with the sense of calling.

A few years ago at the crest of the Allegheny Mountains in Pennsylvania, the Sunshine Special stopped to uncouple an engine. Suddenly, a Pullman car broke loose and hurtled down the hill. For three and a half miles those passengers had a common experience, a democracy of terror and an utter nightmare of fright. Finally the car jumped the track and buried itself in the mountainside. We find ourselves much like these in the car. We are normal persons in a normal car, but suddenly we are caught in something which chills us with a sense of defeat. Writes Edwin Poteat, "In Christ, God enters the world's agony and breaks its downward dash and transmutes it into victory."

The whole process of education is meant to produce an individual who is mature enough to make a responsible choice. We are called to choose. Even within the restrictive barriers of today's catastrophic events and within the many situations which seem to defy the freedom of choice, choice remains. Fosdick's lady was right. Said Dr. Fosdick, "My, but suffering does color your life." "Yes," said she, "but I choose the colors." There is no more important contribution to be made to a growing generation than this sense of responsible freedom, the ability to choose the colors, to live as God's people in this kind of a world. In the end our evangelism, our stewardship, our churchmanship is going to be measured at this point. For to have grown in grace is to

[12] Dietrich Bonhoeffer, *op. cit.*, p. 11 of the Introduction by John Doberstein.

have known God's coming to us, and to have understood that such a love cannot be chained, such a dream cannot be caged. Grow, says the church; grow in mind and in spirit, in total personality. Grow in grace!

SOME SUGGESTIONS FROM OTHERS

Ample materials are available through the Luther League of America, the Lutheran Student Association, and the Lutheran Laymen's Movement providing thoughtful resources for discussions and planning concerning vocations.

"Christian Vocation Days" enjoy increasing popularity. 4-H leaders, county agents, industrial leaders, professional persons and educational leaders are glad to share in developing a thoughtful guide to young people who are planning their occupations. Along with this is the awareness of Christian vocation, the sense of stewardship in all walks of life. Groups such as "The Knights of the Round Table" and Timothy Clubs are active in developing a community of interest which gives inspiration to young people. There is too great a wastage of fine talent and of Christian resourcefulness today.

Where churches are close enough to share resources, great advantage has been gained by promoting joint programs concerning "Preparation for Marriage"; "Christian Careers"; "Recruiting for the Ministry"; "The Christian and His Daily Work."

IV

The Search for Integrity

To Thy Patience in Suffering

+

The memory of a young person kneeling at the altar while the pastor pronounces the prayer of blessing is an appealing and nostalgic one. Included in that prayer is the petition "to thy patience in suffering." To the average fourteen-year-old, that suggests patience during arthritis or some other distant physical ailment. Yet the period of "growing up" is one of those areas of life which is subject to the most poignant suffering.

Young manhood and womanhood is the time of doubts, of searching, of a winsome desire to know self, the world in which men live, and something of an indication of personal destiny. There are personal sufferings which make the physical sufferings of later life pale into insignificance. No church dealing adequately with its young people will overlook the whole area of suffering. "A religious faith that will not concern itself with the vital issues in the life of a person or of a people is a mean and a doomed thing. It is more delusion than an opiate and deserves the scorn which ethically sensitive people are not slow to heap upon it." [1] The words of Dr. Harold Bosley concerning the

[1] Harold Bosley, *Preaching on Controversial Issues* (New York: Harper, 1954), p. 20.

ethical sensitivity of a church are as meaningful in the special area of this chapter.

The confirmed person enters into the life of the congregation. That church at its best is the body of Christ. It is not just the physical organization of a congregation. It is in the church, the suffering sensitive body of God's vibrant wholeness in this world, that we share in the total understanding of the world. No mature faith has been reached until there is a wholeness in personality, until there is an awareness that the church is not for the self-comfort and self-sustenance of a particular group of individuals. It is in the world to keep the Word of God in circulation, to express the love of God in the complexities of men's affairs, and to share the sacraments with their meaning of forgiveness and redemption. It is into this dimensionless area that we must introduce the maturing minds of young men and women confronting the world in terms of their own personal investments of time and talent. In this search for self, and the understanding of personality, many a young person feels caged and trapped. He can only know the frustration of trying to understand self and others. He can sense instinctively the suffering of Bonhoeffer, who in his prison cell could voice the agony of one who has been caged by his captors, and yet has kept untrammeled a conquering faith.

Who Am I?

Who am I? They often tell me
I stepped from my cell's confinement
calmly, cheerfully, firmly,
like a Squire from his country house.

Who am I? They often tell me
I used to speak to my warders
freely and friendly and clearly
as though it were mine to command.

Who am I? They also tell me
I bore the days of misfortune
equably, smilingly, proudly
like one accustomed to win.

Am I then really that which other men tell of?
Or am I only what I myself know of myself?
Restless and longing and sick, like a bird in a cage,
struggling for breath, as though hands were compressing my
  throat,
yearning for colours, for flowers, for the voices of birds,
thirsting for words of kindness, for neighborliness,
tossing in expectation of great events,
powerlessly trembling for friends at an infinite distance,
weary and empty of praying, at thinking, at making,
faint, and ready to say farewell to it all.

Who am I? This or the Other
Am I one person today and tomorrow another?
Am I both at once? A hypocrite before others,
and before myself a contemptible woebegone weakling?
Or is something within me still like a beaten army
fleeing in disorder from victory already achieved?

Who am I? They mock me, these lonely questions of mine.
Whoever I am, Thou knowest, O God, I am Thine! [2]

The factors which keep all too many young people from the
arrival of that final note of victory lie in their feeling of disillusionment as they confront the work and message of the
church. Young people are at once idealistic and impractical.
They would march with banners flying. They want to end
segregation, restore social justice, end divisions between nations
and peoples. For the most part, they are impatient. If you tell
them of the problems which have beset the divisions of churches
throughout the centuries, they want to be done with it now. If

[2] Dietrich Bonhoeffer, *The Cost of Discipleship* (New York: Macmillan,
1949), pp. 15-16.

you discuss some of the social problems that beset men's minds, they want to hurdle them now.

In the midst of this understandable impatience, they see too many persons who have come to terms with life, men and women who have lost the sense of urgency, the fervor and the willingness to adventure. More young people are lost from the Christian cause because of this frustration with what they see than with any conflict with what they have explored with their minds and hearts. They don't believe that their elders believe in this gospel. They think they have regarded the church as though it were another club or organization. So, having lost the sense of the dynamic, of any sense of the church as an organism they suffer, and in their suffering they decide to go it alone.

A little girl came to her father one day with the question, "Dad, what's a museum?" The father patiently explained, but the little fourth-grader quickly exclaimed, "I know that, I was there this afternoon. But what does the word mean?" The father thought a moment and then said "Reach for the dictionary." So they looked it up, and there in the italics was the note that the word "museum" had come from the root, "Muse." With that the father was off in an explanation of the muses, of the ancient idea of inspiration of arts and sciences, poetry and paintings. When he paused to ask, "Do you understand?" the little girl looked quizzical and said, "Yes, but when I was there, I saw a stuffed bear." It is this sense of conflict of what someone has seen in the meaning of an institution and what others see in the actuality that creates a part of the suffering of our generations. We saw the Spirit speaking through men; they may have only seen "the stuffed bears."

When Dr. Paul J. Tillich was confirmed, he reports, "I was told to choose a passage from the Bible as the expression of my personal approach to the biblical message and to the Christian church. Each confirmand was obliged to do so, and to recite a passage before the congregation. When I chose the words, 'Come unto me all ye that are weary and heavy laden,' I was asked with a kind of astonishment, and even irony, why I had chosen this particular passage." [3] Yet, Dr. Tillich, looking back upon the moment, now agrees that he showed an instinctive understanding of the meaning of the Christian faith. It also revealed that awareness of suffering which is a part of every sensitive growing young person.

To these young people the church comes with its message of redemptive love. For "the crucifixion of Jesus set men thinking more than anything else that had ever happened in the life of the human race. And the most remarkable fact in the whole religious thought is this, that when the early Christians looked back and pondered on the dreadful thing that had happened, it made them think of the redeeming love of God. Not simply of the love of Jesus, but of the love of God." [4] It is not to dodge the sufferings of the world, or to ignore the sorrow, or to thunder against the problems or inveigh against the evils that will capture minds. It is when the redeeming love of God is measured over against the evils of mankind, when the sorrows of humankind are held up against the white light of Christ's concerned care, that we capture allegiance.

So this suffering in patience is not a lethargic endurance, a willingness to wait, a retreat from life. Patience is persistence. Patience in suffering is the patient persistent love of a father going out on the road to meet his son, the patient search of a woman for a coin, the patient looking of a shepherd for his sheep.

Dimensions of Faith

We shall have to give young people the dimensions of a restless, creative faith; not a jittery faith, the type of irresponsible, per-

---

[3] Reprinted from *The Shaking of the Foundations*, by Paul Tillich; copyright 1948 by Charles Scribner's Sons; used by permission of the publishers.

[4] Donald Baillie, *God Was in Christ* (New York: Scribners, 1948), p. 184.

spectiveless, uncertain and unpoised action that seems to be the story of so many in our contemporary world. When we think of a person of faith, we ought to think of one ready to handle the unpredictable events of this world with the quiet courage of one who knows that God is trying to get something said in every event.

On the one side we confront those who are desirous only of keeping the status quo. The average young person's discontent has been just here, in the feeling that the church was concerned with the holding of the economic and political security, afraid to venture forth. To such a one the church would seem to be the last remnant of a home to which he could not really go.

On the other side, there seem to be those wistful dreamers who feel splendidly but have no way to implement their emotions.

Somewhere between these two extremes is the creative mind, "a good man who is also wise, a matter of fact realist and a daring idealist, a man in whom two worlds were met, like the voice of a conscience to them in the cool of the morning." To those who have caught anything of the truth in Jesus, there is the scent of the *ought* in the nostrils and the willingness to pursue with restlessness the tough problems of the present. We can't live in a world where the atomic bomb doesn't exist. That's gone. We can't wish for a world where we will conveniently convert all of the atomic energy to peaceful means. That hasn't come. Our young people must go into this world with their restless, creative faith, dissatisfied with the shams of social ignorance, shocked at the stupidity of degrading any human being, horrified at the selfishness that fastens tyranny upon whole generations. The few inches of progress we can ever make is made by those who are aware that God wants them for more than slaves of any system and are restless with this tyranny and cruelty. The Christian faith takes this restlessness and gives a purpose to it, sustains a sensitive conscience which is patient in suffering.

A second description of the quality of faith needed for the world in which suffering young people must live, is an understanding faith. We can live in a universe without understanding, but we cannot live purposeful, useful lives without searching for an understanding. To think so for a moment is to enthrone ignorance and superstition.

The Christian environment ought to be the place where, during these few years, the student has learned more about God, more about the moral structure of this universe, more about the intensely spiritual purposes of this life of ours. Christianity's unique faith in revelation is in this belief that God is coming to man, meeting his unspoken desires, giving himself in our midst. We find in Jesus the God of our lives. So we mean not to be homeless people in this world, but rather those whose home is not a material figment.

Likewise, the Christian faith must enable a young person to understand self. We study our nerve ends, our reactions and responses, but we can still be confused or psychotic. The contribution of the Christian church is to give to its young men and women, and thus to society, persons who are whole persons, well-integrated persons, persons who know how to live the cultured lives of dedicated purpose in a world which makes that increasingly a problem.

Or what have we learned about others? The Christian confronts a world which is striving to learn the meaning of the word "community" and suffers in that struggle. We face no more essential problem than that of human organization. The question today is just how shall we organize life and yet preserve the rights of the individual, the freedom and the worth of the individual. The struggle in our political, social and economic existence comes to focus at this point. Any person who blindly allows a totalitarian power or an institution to take over life has sacrificed the right to freedom. The Christian church contributes to society persons who believe that life can yet be organized on principles guaranteeing dignity to the individual and at the same time basic security for the group.

A third descriptive of the dimensions of the faith we share with young persons caught in the sufferings of the world is a *reverent* faith. We cannot retreat to an old home or security, because it doesn't exist. We go into this new situation with a sense of high reverence, or we shall have missed its full meaning. A man is measured by his reverences. You can tell much about a man by the things that cause him to laugh or to cry, that make him angry or that stir his deepest emotions. A college student, recently being asked to indicate his religious preference, stated, "Gothic." There is a point to keeping something high and vaulted in life, the sense of the holy, which forbids the barrage of cheapness, of degradation and of the easy sham to bleed life dry of its worth and meaning.

The purpose of a pastor is to fit a young person for life, that he might have skills to make a living, faith to build his life, courage to live well beyond his own interests. The Christian faith takes such patterns and fills them with the sense of a creative, understanding, reverent faith which must handle the demanding problems of our times.

To do this we shall have to make a contribution in the development of whole personalities, men and women of integrity. Dr. Karl A. Menninger describes mental health as "the adjustment of human beings to the world and to each other with a maximum of effectiveness and happiness. Not just efficiency or contentment—or the grace of obeying the rules of the game cheerfully. It is all of these together. It is the ability to maintain an even temper, an alert intelligence, socially considered behaviour, and a happy disposition. This, I think, is a healthy mind." [5]

This adjustment becomes increasingly difficult in our world, for it is a world of insecurity. Our situation has been on one

[5] Karl A. Menninger, *The Human Mind* (New York: Alfred Knopf, 1946), p. 1.

hand the superabundance of our own hemisphere, and at the same time the problems of deficiencies and injustices, the problem of suffering and cruelty in the world and the unhealthy fear that we are living on the edge of catastrophe. If it is true that 70 per cent of those in hospitals today are there because of bad mental habits, a major cause can be traced to a type of thinking permitted in maturing years.

Recently two children in a near-by school wrote the following when asked by the teacher to contribute a paragraph concerning what they wanted most of life. "One of America's most dreaded diseases is cancer. It has caused quite a lot of sorrow to many families as it has to mine. Even though I was only about five or six years old, I can still remember what my real mother looked like. Her hair was a golden blonde, and when she had worked very hard, her face would flush a very pretty pink. I noticed when we went to Florida both my mother and father looked worried. Then one day she went to the hospital, and after that we came home. We lived at my sister's home for about a month. One afternoon, when I came back from school, my mother was gone. A few days afterward she died, but I did not know it. After a week had passed, I was told of it. I sincerely hope that someone will find a cure for cancer soon."

The second letter reads: "This experience, I must say, is a very sad one. My mother and father separated about four years ago. For two years, I lived with my mother, but I couldn't stand it without my father, so I came to Buffalo to be with him. My brother joined the army right after they separated, and my sister lives with my mother. I pray to God every night that my mother and father would come together again, but I don't think this will ever happen."

This is the real suffering felt by young people and the challenge toward the building of a real faith so that they are not helpless pawns seemingly shoved by a relentless fate.

A popular magazine recently reported the tragedy of a painter who had spent years in perfecting the techniques of his art and had an overwhelming passion to maintain a memorial for himself. So he painted himself. The tragedy lay in the fact that while his techniques were exceedingly meticulous and clever, he used a cheap oil. Now the portraiture has slid off the canvas and the whole thing is ruined. Here is something of a parable of the problems which we suffer in achieving this adjustment, or peace, or security or wholesomeness, the ambition of the maturing mind. We have discussed values, hopes, and dreams but we have neglected to match our techniques and our methods with our theology, with our basis an oil which has some sense and some meaning to it.

The end of vocation is a development of wholesomeness, integrity, in order to carry out the demands of such a vocation. "As Christians, we know that we have a vocation to do something about the present crisis. Christian principles are clearly involved in the crisis. Christianity is the only agency in our divided world that dares assert that all men are brothers and that God is the Father of all. This profession of faith carries a command, the disregard of which can end only in man's destruction. As Christians of such persuasion we cannot place the interests of a segment of humanity above the higher claims of the whole. In practical terms, this means that no class or state or party can constitute men's highest loyalty. As Edith Cavell said in 1914, 'Patriotism is not enough.' As Christians, we believe that we live in a world of change for material things and that therefore it is impossible to perpetuate the unstable status quo. We believe that human institutions, like the Sabbath, are made for man and that the command to love our neighbor requires the institutions be kept in their instrumental category of serving the needs of men. We believe that the institutions are evil when they cause suffering among men and that then they should be changed—a principle that makes for flexibility and peaceful change. We need in our dynamic world a principle diametrically opposed to the Communist one, that permits neither change nor criticism and subordinates men to its excessive demands. History shows that a high premium is placed upon a point of view that can look upon material things of this world with the considered contempt necessary to keep them from becoming permanent. It is folly to talk about durable peace if we do not know what endures. As Christians, we know the evil nature of man and the surgent necessity of man's salvation from the demon that possesses him when he is desperate and frustrated. These views of the world and of man are the most realistic ones in our day. . . . The time is one full of challenge to all who profess a belief in the fatherhood of God and the brotherhood of man. If this exalted faith cannot release the unexploited resources of intelligence and good will for the benefit of mankind at this critical moment in history, we are indeed lost. In its long and difficult history Christianity has never faced a greater challenge." [6]

To mature in a consciousness of "patience in suffering" is to enter into a growing contact with this suffering world. It is just at this point that the techniques, the plans, the organization and the hopes of the church must bear fruit. To ignore this is to attempt to build a Christian community in a vacuum. Churches which ignore the social situations of their immediate area, whether that be a changing neighborhood in the city or a rural setting, have little right to exist.

When John Oliver Nelson discusses vocation, he speaks of the original and interesting ways in which churches have met the changing situations of life and have actually handled the problems of their environment. Work camps, such as Dr. Herman Keiter's experiments at Hartwick College; the summer camps of the Luther League of America; the projects of various Lutheran

---

[6] Harry R. Rudin in Paul N. Poling (ed.), *God and the Nations* (New York: Doubleday, 1950), pp. 37 ff. Copyright 1950 by the Board of Christian Education of the Presbyterian Church in the United States. Reprinted by permission of Doubleday and Company, Inc.

student groups as well as the camp programs sponsored by the Lutheran World Federation are indicative of the way in which the sore spots of the communities are actually handled by youth groups in the achievement of an understanding that suffering is not just a personal endurance.

These projects are not experiments in humanitarianism, if they are what they are meant to be. They are rather an entry into the suffering of the world.

HOW TO ACHIEVE INTEGRITY

1. *Search for Belonging.* "I am persuaded that nothing can separate me from the love of God which is in Christ Jesus our Lord." Here is the answer to our search for integrity. The task to make this real, vital and important to men and women confronts the church. "The first disciples lived in the bodily presence of Jesus and enjoyed bodily communion with him. In what manner is that communion and fellowship possible for us today? Paul tells us that we are made members of the body of Christ through baptism. But this is such a difficult statement that it requires further elucidation. The church is One Man; it is the body of Christ, but it is also a fellowship of many members." [7] These words of Dietrich Bonhoeffer must have brought him comfort as he waited out the loneliness of his prison-house days and sought for the meaning of belonging.

We live in a time when we have confronted the devastation of many countries and yet most of our members have scarcely known the meaning of loss. We have health, possessions, churches, things. To lose is incredible and incomprehensible. Every pastor knows of the members who have collapsed under the loss of family or friends or possessions or health. Likewise, we have all known persons who have withstood incredible loss, suffering with a sense of understanding and resiliency which defies description.

[7] Dietrich Bonhoeffer, *Life Together*, p. 19.

Unless we are able to impress upon young persons the meaning of loss, and bring them into contact with that loss, they will be unprepared for life in such a world. Overprotected children and young people shielded from the reality of life produce adults who are unprepared for the harsh possibilities of existence. Write Drs. English and Pearson: "In the process of growth, it is important that we learn that *life is uncertain,* that *it has vicissitudes* and that *we need to invest* as much of our interest in as many people and in as many things as we reasonably can." Samuel Johnson said that "we must work at making friends and we must keep our friendships constantly in repair." In other words, we must be prepared for loss—not necessarily dwell upon it or brood about it, but be emotionally and rationally prepared for it. There is no reason why we should not accomplish this attitude of mind with the proper training." [8]

In discussions, in conferences, in friendships, in the excellence of preaching, in the vastness of liturgical understanding, in the warm intimacy of prayer, in the ministry of the church in health and sickness, in the social thrust of the church into the community in which it lives, in every conceivable way this concept of belonging must be emphasized, rooted and grounded in love.

Young people in West Germany are busy giving aid and sustenance to their brethren in East Germany: this is a sense of belonging. Youth groups in cities have shared in field trips in which they have become aware of their own city and its own social sore spots: this is the sense of belonging. Luther Leagues in rural areas have been busily engaged in conducting camps and vacation schools, learning to understand the problems of maintaining rural churches throughout our country: this is the sense of belonging. Frankly, most youth groups in churches need to find the creative opportunity to put to work in actual practice the principle underlying their liturgies, their worship, their hymns and their articles of faith.

[8] Oliver S. English and G. H. J. Pearson, *op. cit.,* p. 386.

2. *See All Things.*

> All things come of Thee, O God,
> And of Thine own have we given Thee.

So we sing concerning possessions—possessions which are not just economic. We are whole persons only when we live in a knowing awareness of this world. It is at this point that the church must conceive of its task in the same spirit as the prophets and the disciples. The prophets regarded their mission as the whole man, in the entirety of his life and habits. Jesus spoke of the same principles. The Pharisee was condemned because he was holding up religious practices as the only criterion for his righteousness. The men who were called "whited sepulchers" and condemned because they refused to take in earnest the meaning of their faith were those who could not see religion as the whole of existence. "Why all this stress on behaviour? Because, as I think you have realized, the present time is of highest importance—it is time to wake up to reality. Every day brings God's salvation nearer." (J. B. Phillips' paraphase of Romans 13:11). The church continuously needs to keep its young people in touch with the arts, the professions, the other countries of the world, the needs of mankind. We send our men and women around the world in military service. We want to send them with a faith that has great horizons. Recently, General Charles I. Carpenter, Air Force Chief of Chaplains, called upon churches to give increased attention to providing religious resources for servicemen. If present trends continue, said the general, one million men will be going into service each year, and one million will be coming out—after two or four years of service. If these men come back with an insight into only the lower life of countries, our foreign policy and the entire character of our country can change in time.

You can put millions of dollars into foreign missions, but unless something can be done to influence the lives of the young men and women who go into the armed forces, you are throwing money away, says the chaplain. Churches should inform their members serving overseas about mission stations and native churches. In this way the servicemen will be able to keep in touch with religious activities.

The church makes no finer contribution to growing minds than this breaking through of the pigeon-holing of life—this shattering of little cultural patterns—this breaking down of social barriers and indifference. Churches have a way of thinking of themselves as unimportant, or little, or distant, or insignificant, and thereby losing a sense of belonging to the kingdom.

3. *The Strength of Patience and Persistence.* The virtue of patience is not lethargy, not doleful waiting, not "sit down, men of God, the kingdom he will bring, there's nothing you can do." Patience is degraded by such distortions. Patience is the persistence of love, the persistence of a patient father, the patience of the atonement, the patience of the kingdom. It is the patience that can only be had by those who believe in the redeeming love of God. Only such believing can afford to be patient.

This is never more effectively demonstrated than at the point where we involve men and women in the patient processes of witnessing to this faith. Evangelism is reaching out to encourage men and warm hearts. Stewardship is the encouragement of wisely sharing gifts and talents. Education is the leading out from ignorance, prejudice and shame the minds of those in Sunday school and in higher education. Worship is the free opening of life to the full strength of "waiting upon the Lord." Such are the results of an awareness of and dedication to the patient love of God which we know through the Gospels.

A few years ago in our congregation, I called upon a woman who had suffered much throughout many years. She was one of those persons who was confined to her room for so long that it was hard for any of us to remember when she had not been there. One Christmas time, I laughingly asked her what Santa Claus was going to bring her. Her eyes twinkled and she said, "I would like most of all to have a chance to go downstairs once more for dinner." There it was—staring at you, the deep down desire—and I'd brought it on myself. Conferences with the family and the doctor revealed that it could be done if there were strong young men who could gently and slowly carry her down the steep stairway. It was discussed with a youth group at the church. Two tall young men volunteered and on the next Sunday after church these men fulfilled their task. Late in the afternoon they returned to carry her back to her bed. For several years this went on every month until the day came when she was too weak to be moved. Looking back on their experience, these young men testified that this was the first time they had physically touched suffering. They knew of it—they had an academic appreciation, but to actually hold in their arms this suffering skeletal form of a woman and carry her up or down a stairway gave to them a new sense of gentleness. They felt better prepared for the exigencies of life, more alert to life's needs, better prepared for marriage. They would now appreciate the whole of life with a new gentleness, because they had learned "the patience of suffering."

4. *Meditation.* We need to challenge lonesome young people with the meaning of quiet. It isn't that they think of themselves as lonely, but every man sooner or later confronts the loneliness of making a personal decision. There is never a more isolated spot. That is the time when it seems, as Kierkegaard said, "that we had come to that island so barren that there is no place to hide."

We Protestants need to tell our young people the meaning of silence, the quiet of worship, the leadership necessary for prayer.

Roman Catholics have been given mechanical means to guide their prayers. We need none of these, and yet there is the easy temptation to imitate. What is necessary is the kind of leadership in studying the meaning of prayer and suggestions in the building of a healthy, intellectually honest personal devotion. Edward R. Murrow reports that in his interviews with men and women concerning their personal faith most of them confessed that one of their most difficult tasks was setting down in logical order the things they believed. There will be many techniques, many ways in which this is accomplished, many ways in which we can give guidance. One of the most important is in this development of the understanding of quiet, of rest and prayer. I am impressed by the numbers of young men who have had to endure the tortures of long months of separation from their families, of prisoners who have been held in enemy camps, and of the need that these young people had for a mature faith and prayer life.

In a survey entitled "When the Going Gets Tough," Dr. Menninger[9] reports these statistics:

Officers	Enlisted Men	
53%	63%	felt that prayer helped a lot
15%	1%	felt that prayer helped some
6%	6%	felt that prayer gave little or no help
26%	18%	did not think of it

The tragedy of so much thinking about prayer in our time and of meditation is that it is regarded in a sentimental, unreal attitude. We need the disciplining awareness of God's power, the knowledge of grace, the discipline of being still, of thinking, of praying, of worship.

5. *Wholeness*. Healthiness is wholeness. Let me quote from that peerless friend, Oscar Blackwelder:

[9] William C. Menninger, *Psychiatry in a Troubled World* (New York: Macmillan, 1945), p. 100.

To be a person means to be an all-round man.
An all-round man is a man of integrity—he is not fractional.
An all-round man is a holy man, he has a controlling power
   for his life;
An all-round man is a person of culture.[10]

Too many times men and women think of piety as a devotion
to a religious principle that does not carry over into the whole
of life. By the same token, we develop loyalty to a congregation
and not to the kingdom of God; to a denomination and not to
Christ; to a principle of practice or organizational preference
instead of to the organizing principle of love. Says Dr. Pearson,[11]
"The progress of events is showing us quite clearly that if our
concept of loyalty is too small, we shall all come to grief. We
cannot be loyal to only one person, to one family, or even to
one country. Our concept of loyalty must extend to everyone
if we are to be citizens of the world. Christianity has always had
inherent in it the concept of greater love, but few people have
considered how much we should be loyal to ourselves and how
much to all mankind. We have undoubtedly made the mistake
of loving causes and concepts more than persons. Unfortunately,
at present it seems that our loyalty to mankind is being developed
through fear and force rather than through idealistic teaching."
Loyalty to the whole is learning the ever-widening circle of
interest once we have placed ourselves within the scope and
meaning of the kingdom.

6. *The Good Cheer of Creative Imagination.* A famous
preacher once said that the difference between preachers is in
imagination. Perhaps so. It is really the difference between all
persons. Imagination is not wistfully imagining the unreal. It
is the miracle of using the real and conceiving its true worth and

[10] Oscar Blackwelder in *Reality in Preaching* (Philadelphia: Muhlenberg,
   1942).
[11] O. S. English and G. H. J. Pearson, *op. cit.*, p. 386.

value in the light of God's grace. Jesus called the disciples and with striking imagination set their hands to great tasks, tore them loose deliberately, taught them the discipline of following. It was no easy thing. It required imagination to understand. They did not suddenly drift to Pentecost. They took a long trek of discipleship, learning the cost and meaning of it. For much of that way they were dulled by their own fears. When they were laid hold upon, when they realized that it hath not yet appeared what they might be, that no one had ever imagined the fulness of Christ's power, life began to make sense and they had power.

For all too many persons, the church has been concerned with little ends in little ways. Only when it stretches its meaning, when with bold imagination it is concerned with the kingdom, do we begin to produce whole holy men and women who are the vehicles for God's grace and power, who find the newer meanings of life in the midst of suffering. The handling of problems of narcotics addiction, alcoholism, the problems which are variously termed as "delinquency" are all in the area which demand imagination and creative ability. They are at the place where, as a report on activities of a parish in East Harlem indicates, "these young people in whom are stirring the seeds of concern and militancy have not yet decided fully to play God's game. But as long as they exist in conscious dedication to God's purpose and are fortified by communions in which God's grace shines through in spite of dirty windows, there is hope that they will be the local foci of community in which they live." [12]

In the end, it will be only by the good cheer of imaginative Christian faith at it deepest and best that the suffering which youth knows can be won to the dedication of the whole life. "Be done with these worries," said Luther, chiding Melanchthon. He needed to find a way to do it too. And if you look closely at him you discover that it is that incomparable sense of good

[12] East Harlem Parish Report for 1954.

85

humor by which he was able to woo mankind to an understanding of Christ's love. Here is the "good cheer" of which Jesus spoke when he gave hope and confidence to mankind. "Hope means the presence of the future, or more precisely, it is one of the ways in which what is merely future and potential is made vividly present and actual to us. Hope is the positive, as anxiety is the negative, mode of awaiting the future." [13]

There is a story, heard first in London, of a young pianist, cruelly wounded in the war, coming to consciousness and discovering the loss of his right arm. For months, he languished in heartbroken despondency and mental suffering. Then with the slow return of health, a friend brought him to Sir Walford Davies, the distinguished composer. Sir Walford took him for a walk across the campus to a cathedral and, entering, asked the young man to wait there for a while. He went to the organ and played for half an hour. When he returned, the young man looked up almost bitterly and said, "Why do you torture me like this? Once I could play like that." Sir Walford spoke gently, "You can play like that again, young man. For the last half hour I played with the left hand and the pedals." The man who told the story said, "I do wish that you could have been here last evening. You would have heard him play with the London Symphony Orchestra, 'Ravel's Concerto for the Left Hand.'" So, to quote Brunner again, "As the fate of the human organism is dependent on the supply of oxygen, so the fate of humanity is dependent on its supply of hope."

This is Jesus dealing with mankind. It is his "Be of good cheer, for I have overcome the world." It is his "Father, forgive them" and "Into thy hands I commend my spirit." Only that person of hope, born of an understanding of the gospel, will be able to meet the demands placed upon the human being in this hour. This is the maturing that must come after confirmation or the end is a

[13] Emil Brunner, *Eternal Hope* (Philadelphia: Westminster, 1954), p. 7.

disintegration of personality and a loss of purpose for life. With this hope, born of good cheer, is the sense of eternal destiny of belonging to a kingdom, of participation in the community of the righteous. Then, to be patient in suffering is to live with a defense against the unremitting despair of nihilism and cynicism, aware of the meaning of forgiveness, caught in the understanding of a redeeming love and held to the creative use of God's ministry in every difficulty.

SOME SUGGESTIONS FROM OTHERS

The projects of the Luther League of America are of special importance in this area, especially in view of their conviction that their work camps are not to be regarded as service projects. There is none of the "do-goodism" about this but rather the consciousness that this is an exploration of Christian truth in actual social situations. The same idea can be expressed in numerous ways in any parish, anywhere. The important thing is not just what a group decides to do, but rather what a group decides to achieve in what it is doing.

One rural church reports special groups which have met in the summertime to study the Bible and great Christian teachings in a more thorough way. They have explored great devotional readings and have found within the group the resources of prayer and meditation which have enabled them to understand better both themselves and their need of spiritual resources.

One pastor reports a special folder which he keeps for each young person in his parish. In it he keeps the results of interviews, impressions through the years, suggestions which may enable him to meet the young person in a personal way and give honest assistance in a time when there is a basic struggle concerning choices, decisions, or a meeting of those situations which might leave them defeated.

V

Possessing Our Possessions

And the Blessed Hope of Everlasting Life

+

The recurring note of the Christian life is the reality of hope. Man can strip himself of many things in this world and he will find life uncomfortable, but still tolerable. But divest him of hope and he is ready for the desperation which characterizes so much of modern madness. There is no greater gift that the Christian can receive than this gift of hope. St. Paul knew that. "Who can separate us from the love of Christ?" he writes. "Shall tribulation, or distress, or persecution, . . . or sword? . . . Nay, in all these things we are more than conquerors. . . . For I am persuaded, that neither death, nor life, nor angels, nor principalities, nor powers, nor things present, nor things to come nor height, nor depth, nor any other creature, shall be able to separate us from the love of God, which is in Christ our Lord." There is a confident faith which breathes the maturity of hope. About such a life is an unconquerable spirit. This is the desire of every maturing Christian.

All of this is relevant for the confirmand, who prays for the blessed hope of everlasting life, is praying for more than a hope at the time of death. This terminal hope has immediate responsibilities, a fact which youth must understand. It is the possession of the Christian, granted by God's grace; it is known by God's power; it is possessed at once in the individual. The blessedness of hope is in the awareness that we are a part of the community of the righteous. Being in that community is not a sudden act at the time of death, but a present possession which needs to be possessed now. Death becomes a startling transition. Death is the radical cessation of life here. It is not the cessation of the community. That person who lives well in the community, whose faith and hope is significant in the community of suffering and joy, pain and sorrow now is in the community.

The paradox of this belonging to the community is well put by Luther. "Do not recommend to me peace and unity when thereby God's Word is lost, for then eternal life and everything else would be lost. In this matter there can be no yielding nor giving way, no, not for love of you or any other person, but everything must yield to the Word, whether it be friend or foe. The Word was given unto us for eternal life and not to further outward peace and unity. The Word and doctrine will create Christian unity or fellowship. Where they reign all else will follow. Where they are not no concord will ever abide. Therefore do not talk to me about love and friendship, if that means breaking with the Word, or the faith, for the Gospel does not say love brings eternal life, God's grace, and all heavenly treasures, but the Word." [1]

A LAYMAN'S THEOLOGY

One of the problems of the church is that theology is thought to be the possession of a profession. That invades even the ministry. Pastors apologize at times by saying, "Although I am not a theologian. . . ." In heaven's name, who will be the theologian in that community? Theology is not a professional possession belonging to a certain vocabulary or technology. The theologian "per se" performs a useful and essential service to the

[1] Martin Luther in *Day by Day We Magnify Thee*, p. 384.

church by his scientific awareness of the nature of life. What the theologian as such gives to life is also a possession of all persons. His relationship to the churches is as the architect to the resident, or the mechanic to the car. Yet appreciation of the house is not a sole possession of the architect. As a matter of fact, the architect may know the construction of the house, but the appreciation of the life of the home is another matter. What the church wants of its laymen is not necessarily the important technician. The church does want the lover of truth, the seeker for knowledge, the growing maturing Christian individual.

A luminous passage in Dr. Kantonen's book, *The Theology of Evangelism,* is relevant: "Christianity spread because it was essentially a lay movement in which every member was a missionary. Wherever they were or wherever they went, they spoke a good word for Christ. They lived for Him—they died for Him. It is significant that the very word *layman* is derived from *laos,* meaning people, the word which the New Testament uses to designate the messianic people, the royal priesthood of believers. To be a layman is thus the highest honor which the New Testament knows. It is to be a kingdom man, a Christ man. The distinction between the minister and the layman is utterly insignificant compared with the distinction between being 'in Christ' or 'out of Christ.' The only thing that ultimately matters is to be 'in Christ,' a member of His body and His kingdom, doing His work, whatever one's other calling may be.

"This insight must be recaptured in all its vitality if the church is to awake from its complacent isolationism to fulfil its mission in the world today. In a world in which large sections of the population even in so-called Christian countries are no longer even nominally Christian, and in which militant anti-Christian forces are rampant, the church dare not merely mark time. The whole church, from local parishes and general church bodies to the highest levels of interdenominational co-operation, must emerge as a world-wide evangelizing fellowship, with a realistic strategy and a rededicated will to carry out its central purpose to win every area of life for Christ. To this end, every man and woman in our pews must be enlightened to the true meaning of the Christian fellowship and consecrated to the tasks of the universal priesthood. They must become the means by which men in every stratum of society, from the ranks of unskilled labor to the sophisticated intelligentsia of the universities, are confronted with the living Christ." [2]

An interesting story is told of an elderly couple sitting on their broken-down porch of a little house in Oklahoma. There they had worked, struggled, scratched in the hot dust of the plains for years and had barely managed to exist. Now, as they sat rocking and thinking of life's hardships, trucks came down the roadway, bringing strange-looking machinery. The men began to work and within time, a man walked over to the porch and pointed to the oil well and its gushing wealth and said, "Grandpa, you're rich." The old man kept on rocking and said simply, "And to think of it, Ma, we've been sitting on it all of these years." In a sense this is what happens to so many people, reared in the church, yet coming into conflict with vocabulary, terms, pictures, ideas which make them think that they have come into conflict with religion itself.

Many of these persons go out to scratch in the hot dust and gravel of our time, coming up with all manner of notions. Chiefly, they needed just to drill deep where the accrued wealth of apostles, prophets, saints and martyrs had brought the revealed Word of God, kept in its richness through the years until at long last there might be ready for our own needs this meaning of God's concern and care. They had but to possess their possessions.

[2] T. A. Kantonen, *The Theology of Evangelism* (Philadelphia: Muhlenberg, 1954), pp. 96 f.

THE TRAGEDY OF SUPERSTITION

This is the tragedy we confront, of allowing growing persons to be content with a childhood memory, permitting our churches to be the refuge of the unsearching, unpossessing inheritors. Somehow, we shall have to go out to possess the land we have already possessed. In the very first Knubel-Miller lectures, Dr. Walton Harlowe Greever tells of a man whose only knowledge of religion is that the preacher is in favor of God. Here, said Dr. Greever, is the pathos of the situation.

John Oliver Nelson tells the story of an ancient parish church, where as the worshipers entered they bowed to a certain wall beside the door. Nobody knew why but the practice continued. Only when the workmen scraped the wall for repainting was it discovered that long ago a picture of Christ had been there. Painted over decades ago, the picture caused everyone to nod in reverence. Even though the reason for such behavior becomes lost, the custom continues. But after a while the custom becomes superstition and corrodes life. So the pathos becomes tragedy.

Here are active adult churchfolk who have an ancient memory of somebody called Jonah and no concept of a magnificent portrayal of God's international concern. Adult Christians know a little fact or two about Job and his boils but they have no understanding of one of the world's greatest studies in the whole problem of suffering. Culturally literate persons in our midst still look at religion as though it were escape from life instead of a deep entanglement with this world's agony.

As a matter of fact, a survey of college pastors reveals that most students who have been reared in the atmosphere of the church complain that they were left without a continuing religious experience. They were taught certain facts or stories, left with certain impressions and now, because they have come into conflict with certain words or word-concepts, they think they have to come at odds with religion itself.

"Sir Walter Moberly, writing in his searching analysis of

higher education, *The Crisis in the University* says: 'The cultural failure of the universities is seen in the students. In recent years large numbers of these have been apathetic and have had neither wide interests nor compelling convicitions. Whatever the cause, the university today lives and moves and has its being in a moral and cultural fog.' Let no one condemn our schools and colleges for their indifference to religion unless he sees himself under like condemnation. For are not students and youth generally part of the world we have made? Do they not reflect their elders' attitudes and practices? We too, share their working philosophy and much of their way of living, and like it. As for churches and church folk, would you say that we give the impression of being excited about the truth we profess? . . . Thomas Mendip in Christopher Fry's play, *The Lady Is Not for Burning:*

> Oh, be disturbed,
> Be disturbed, madam, to the extent of a tut,
> And I will thank God for all civilization
> This is my last throw, my last poor gamble
> On the human heart." [3]

Gordon W. Allport points out that there are three stages in the development of a mature faith. The first is that of raw credulity, most clearly seen in a child who believes what he hears. To him words are as good as facts. Some people keep a faith in this state—childish, authoritarian, irrational. A second stage is the eruption of doubts and the disruption that occurs when one is unable to reconcile new areas of life with what seem to be improbabilities of the past. Out of this seedbed of development could grow a mature faith. Left in that area, life becomes a place of cynicism and we continue in that adolescence of doubt.

"Mature belief, the third stage, grows painfully out of the

[3] David MacLennan, *op. cit.*, p. 154.

alternating doubts and affirmations that characterize productive thinking." It is this growing, maturing faith which must be the end result of all of our congregational relationships, giving a dynamic to knowledge, an *elan* to facts, an organizing of life with the quality of vocation.

THE INTERPLAY OF GROWTH AND EMOTION

To many persons there has always seemed to be something of a conflict between those who believed in the educational growth of a religious faith and those who insisted on an emotional experience. In fact, there needs to be a synthesis. Dr. Reu insisted: "The life of the mature congregation is primarily a life of faith. Through faith it has grasped Jesus Christ and has become a Christian congregation; in faith it must embrace Christ anew if it is to maintain its character as such; and all of its activities must grow out of such faith to be acceptable to God." Having accepted such a statement, the church has many times been content to grasp, but not to grasp anew.

For that matter, much educational matter in the church school has dealt with materials which allowed no great emotional pull toward religious growth. All too many times, religious education has been degraded with juvenile character education, devoid of any great compulsion upon the individual. Chad Walsh quotes a student, "I suppose that someday when I am older and my mind is too tired to ask 'why,' and when I am weak enough to submit, I shall accept Christianity in the weakness of my old age as I did in the innocence of my childhood." It is to such young people that the church must come with an understanding of the need to possess our possessions.

TOWARDS MATURITY

Here are some of the general steps in the striving for this maturing personal and congregational life.

1. *A Time for Rethinking*

The confessions of the church have come to us because men have thought reverently concerning their faith and then ventured boldly to articulate that faith. That heritage is no magic touchstone. It needs to be rethought in each generation in the terms, the environment, and the thought-patterns of the present. This is the responsibility of every parish. It is not a professional task. It is the possessing of the possessions.

For instance, every congregation, large or small, can have a Board of Education comprising personnel of the church which intelligently attacks the problem of the education of the members. It is not just a matter of Sunday school or auxiliary. It is a matter of a parish meeting the increasing needs of the entire family. Unless we do that, God is degraded into the "man upstairs" and religion has become nothing more than a necessary superstition which is tolerated because people want to be on the safe side.

It is at this point that young people rebel and it is there that religion loses "its blessed hope." In the early church there were long periods of waiting until men and women were permitted to enter into the full life of the congregation. Some denominations and groups have attempted to do this in our own time. All groups need to adapt this concept of preparation. The programs of adult education which crowd city high schools in the evenings, the development of activities in 4-H groups and teen-age group-programs all look toward the leading of adults into a conscious awareness of resources necessary for their situation.

Precisely this is incumbent upon the church. That church which has felt that its adult Bible class is not reaching as many persons, need not—must not—take a defeatist attitude. Once upon a time, that class was an innovation. We need now to survey our situation and create the evening or extra-curricular programs of adult education.

In the end, as Dr. Buttrick once said, "Christ laid siege to a few hearts along the stray road. Instead of giving a whitewash of religion, he decided to live with a few individuals until they caught the real spirit of what he was trying to do." The illiteracy of large numbers of people concerning the thought of Christian leaders, the books which have set men's feet to marching, the meaning of the liturgies which have lifted men's lives, the strength of their prayers which have united men's hands, the majesty of the great statements of faith which have given high-vaulted hopes to men's living, need to be rethought and re-explored.

The techniques for all of this are as varied as the individuality of congregations. One group uses a Great Books motif. Another tries it with luncheon meetings. A third has evening classes. Another has been holding neighborhood meetings. Each man has to adapt the techniques to his situation. The important emphasis is that each congregation has to be an energy point, a place of educational experience, where a maturing Christian faith is inspired in a service of worship, impressed in fellowship and expressed as an alert conscience. The only church worthy of its name is going to rethink its faith with each generation. This is the present impact of the knowledge of a blessed hope.

2. The Awareness of Tension

When we begin to possess our possessions, we establish a tension. Every pastor who thinks courageously of his work with young people will have to ask whether he ever sent a young man away sorrowing, beleaguered with enough questions to return for understanding. Only with such a tension will there ever be a growing edge, creating a new generation of Christian thinkers. We'd better not try to enslave them with thoughts of discovering a quiet peace. No person was ever lured to give himself to greatness on such terms. It is at this point where we may be able to preach, to teach, to challenge, assisting young men and women to rethink their faith in terms which have maturity.

A recent visit to a home for older people is a case in point. A gentleman in a near-by bed recognized that I was a pastor and asked that I say a prayer for him. I assured him that I would do so, but suggested that he say one first. He replied that he knew no prayer. Encouraging him, I assured him that he must know one prayer. After a moment, this ninety-two-year-old man smiled and began to say, "Now I lay me down to sleep, I pray the Lord my soul to keep." It was beautiful and heart-touching —and sad. All of these years and this was the only prayer. All of the decades and yet it was a prayer once learned. The whole adventure of maturing prayer-experience that had been missed. With a lifetime of possible companionship with one's Lord and Master, now at this hour of need there was only the blessed remembrance of childhood prayer.

There are numbers of our members who have been unable to think with any larger sense of prayer, who have thought with nostalgia of the happy security of their childhood and have been unable to recreate a new sense of security in the exploding world in which they live.

No problem so puzzles young people as the obvious injustices that flourish in the world. The iniquitous do prosper. The evil man does get ahead. No immature faith can withstand this challenge.

Yet in this incredible world an incredible fact has occurred. Christ has come! The meaning of life is in a God who has broken through this universe to bring to us something of the knowledge of self, an awareness of sin and a blessed hope.

"As soon as a man steps right out of the realm of distributive justice, and sets on one side the idea that rewards and penalties are a clue to the understanding of the divine government of the world, not only is he given an entirely new attitude to such sufferings and deprivations as may be his own lot, but also it

becomes possible for him at least to begin to see all the dire sufferings of men—all the long anguish and travail and frustration
of history—in a new light. There will remain, even so, much
darkness and mystery—much to wring the heart, much to call for
faith—but at least it now becomes possible to believe, nay to
know, that God is using it all, and will use it all, to build up a
kingdom of persons in relationship—a kingdom whose governing
principle is not, I repeat, 'justice' and awarding of prizes or
penalties, but a sacrificial self-giving which knows and desires no
other good thing than to be at one with God, and with all persons,
in love. As leading up to that consummation in the divine
kingdom which lies beyond history, all that men have suffered
so unequally and so perplexingly in history will at least be seen
to have been fully worth while, calling for no nice compensating
adjustments on the part of God, and no regrets on the part of
men." [4]

3. The Need of an Awakened Interest in Theology

Dean Willard Sperry once wrote of worship, "a service of
worship does not guarantee an immediate religious experience. . . .
But it furnishes occasion for that recollection in tranquility by
which we possess ourselves permanently of the certitudes which
have been ours. Worship is the poetic resolution of the riddle
of the expedient absences of the Divine. It furnishes both the
occasion and the method for this reflective comprehension of life.
It reilluminates the common day by its meditative recovery of
the celestial light." This presupposes that we have had satisfying
experiences through the years which arouse satisfaction. "Prayer
at its best, like music at its best, has meanings that can never be
put into words. It is for this reason that sacred formulae of
prayer, familiar since childhood but in a language unknown to
the worshiper, may be for him full of meaning, and of meaning

[4] H. H. Farmer, *God and Man* (Nashville: Abingdon, 1952), pp. 198 f.

more profound than a literal translation of the words could express." [5]

Men of vast areas of religious experience have recognized that there can be a satisfying response from an established ritual even when it is not translated into the language of the worshiper. What we are concerned about in our time is the continuing retranslation into the emotional life of the worshiper and his intellectual comprehension of this "reflection of certainty."

Such certitudes are not just emotional experiences. They are the grasping of the meaning. A study of the concepts to which we readily participate in the Common Service reveals this need of a growing religious experience. We have possessed the liturgical expression through the years. It is the congealed product of centuries of experience. It has outreaches which satisfy. Yet it can be to some a professionalized methodology, to others merely "the opening service," to yet others a kind of dramatic setting.

One can look at a portrait and think of it in terms of artistic technique. The skill of the artist impresses, even though the subject of the portrait itself is nameless. An entirely different experience occurs if one knows the subject. The recent controversy concerning a portrait of Churchill is a case in point. Emotions were immediately aroused since men were not only looking at the skill of the artist but rather looking through the portrait to the personality of the subject. Had he caught the real Mr. Churchill? Something of the same experience has to be the concern of the Christian church. We can never be satisfied with the correct and orderly preservation of the symbols of faith as though they are museum-pieces. It has to be a shared experience, a maturing satisfying fact, being laid hold on, as well as going through. One has to see through a call to worship,

---

[5] Willard L. Sperry, *Reality in Worship* (New York: Macmillan, 1925), p. 177.

a confession of sins, a Gloria in Excelsis, if that experience is vital.

It is this which we can call by any name but which is in the end a theological concern. The congregation which is content to impose forms of worship upon people, to become immersed with rigidities in worship, in organizational form or in vocabulary, or in ecclesiastical millinery has denied itself the energizing life of the gospel. The gospel flows through but is not captured in these forms. The gospel energizes them, is seen through and found in communal expression, but is never limited to these historic practices. The more we gather our people together to think of that which we do, the more we give them a common concern for every need of life.

A commentator of the contemporary religious scene wrote, "The tragedy and the paradox of our situation is that these religious giant sellers in fiction and 99 out of 100 non-fiction books sold under the banner of religion address themselves only to the spiritual comforts available to the Christian of sure faith, and not at all with the religious foundations of that faith. They concern themselves more with man than with man's concerns. Faith today has a thousand voices; religion flowers in silence.

"The powder of prettiness and the pettiness that has sifted down upon the shoulders of the Old Testament prophets and the New Testament fathers has served to smother them as human beings, and to take them, heels dragging in their own greatness, out of the arena of history. The prophet who was thrown down a well, the power and rugged old counselor of four kings of Judah, the man who paved the way for the whole Christian religion . . . lost to us as historical figures.

"Today the most literate and educated nation in the world is suffering from a tragic and pathetic illiteracy . . . an ignorance of the historical foundations of his own religion."

We are not going to assist men and women to possess their

101

heritage of faith by an attitude of protectiveness. We must be out in the fight, facing the challenge of the issues of the day as they confront the church. We shall have to think with them at the growing edge, at the controversial edge and at a moment when we may not be able to come up with absolute answers.

There is nothing that will be asked more than honest thinking, freedom from cant, from pat answers, from the kind of dodging that many times characterizes the popular impression of religion. Harold Cooke Phillips once said he had to believe all the more in God because there was a war, since the war showed again how impossible it was to live on the plane of immorality. "If there was not a war, I could not believe in God for man had so long flaunted what we had believed was the moral worth of God." And Niebuhr adds, "We were not able to believe that Hitler was so bad because we had not believed in the sinfulness of sin, the hellishness of hell and the brutality of man." Now we know and we confront this every day. We have discovered that merely dressing up the environment will not protect us from communism, nor will deluding ourselves by economic methods turn the trick. We will be effective only when we have been able to create in growing minds the conscious awareness that religion has to deal with life at its outreach.

Nothing should disturb the church as much in our time as the ease with which so many persons who are otherwise intelligent go running after every little idea which tags on the name of religion. Men and women throw together numbers of ideas about God and call it religion. It's a discouraging thing but then, maybe it has been our fault. Only when we plumb the depths of the great confessions of the Christian faith in the midst of the tensions of our time, only when we sense the hunger of this broken world for the message of faith and hope in terms which grapple with our problems, will we enable growing minds to lay hold on truth to actually possess that which they have hitherto inherited.

4. *More Opportunities for Study*

Somehow the churches must continue to provide more opportunities for the discussion of and conferring about the whole
work of the Christian church. All of us know the frustration
of trying to plan programs in the busy schedules of overworked
individuals. Yet within the whole structure of the church there
must be this opportunity to concern the membership of the
church with the controversial, the yeasty and fermentive situations of our communities as well as with an exploration of the
total meaning of the faith. Unless this is done there will be a
cleavage between pulpit and pew and a loss of the imperative
which has been the birthright of the Protestant church.

Wrote a young person in the *New York Times*, "I think I
speak for youth when I say we are sick to death of platitudes
and cliches, of flag-waving and heroic attitudes, of Red scares and
patriotism that is talked rather than felt, of soothing talk and
accusations, of political parties and political corruption, and all
of the other paraphernalia which are our unsavory heritage. No,
Mr. Editor, it is not ours that is the lost generation—it is yours.
We only ask that you don't take us down with you." [6]

So, as Paul Scherer once wrote, "We have got to love the
world enough to defy it again, exasperate it, make its smug
complacencies miserable, sting its calloused soul alive, rub to the
quick again these flesh and blood situations, and lay them
quivering on the human conscience. What seems to me to be
the most subversive of all of our hopes at the present time is the
most irresistible tendency to fade into the general landscape for
fear of running counter to something in it so that our voices may
sound precisely like the voice of the man in the street, and the
methods we proclaim are the methods he fashions. We have got

[6] Samuel M. Shoemaker, "Youth Has Its Chance," in Gordon Speer (ed.),
Talks to Youth (Nashville: Abingdon, 1949), p. 111.

to keep alive the tensions between man's word and God's Word." [7]

To do this there will have to be groups at which the Christian faith is discussed in the framework of the local situation, drilling deep into the depths of life and thought to discover the resources to handle the situations of our time. For instance, in the discussion concerning juvenile delinquency and youth problems, most of them are held up against the behavior pattern of another generation. Most letters to the editor have comments from people who urge a return to the "practice of taking the youngsters to the woodshed." Whatever the answer to the serious problem of vandalism and hoodlumism, it can't be solved by such procedures. The judge in one of the local courts who urged parents to "kick their teeth in" was resorting to the same easy tendency that men resort to when they become frustrated with a difficult situation and feel the urge to try violence or an attempted solution using the background of another generation.

All of this is a symptom of our ignorance of great redemptive faith. We have no knowledge that the statements which we have confessed stake out the ground where we can be laid bare to the power to handle life. When the church is brave enough in its social concern to say the things which it actually believes in its creeds, it will win the allegiance of mankind. When it is bold enough to be in truth what it says it is in its historic origins it will challenge mankind to new courage. Dr. Charles Ranson, general secretary of the International Missionary Council, insists, "The answer to Marxism, the ultimate Christian answer, is a theological one. The answer is not a social theory—not even in a declaration of moral absolutes. Only by a proclamation of the truth that the world has a Lord, a Judge, and a Saviour, Jesus Christ, who stands outside and judges history, can human rights ultimately be safeguarded and human justice ultimately achieved."

[7] Paul E. Scherer, *For We Have This Treasure* (New York: Harper, 1945), p. 125.

This is the blessed hope that has great significance in our present situation.

5. More Opportunities to Express Faith

Young people can mature when they find themselves. The church, possessing its own possessions, must find the courage to probe deep into the articles of its faith, and deal with contemporary situations, or it will lose these idealistic (and many times unrealistic) young people. A church which confronts the problem of segregation with timidity and compromise will have difficulty giving a moral incentive to young people. The church which faces situations of growing tensions with cowardice will save an argument and lose a generation. The church which is false to the best meaning of its own faith will lose its reason for existence. The Lutheran church bears the name of one who on many occasions said and did things in the political and social situation of his time which we would not agree with in our own time. The important fact remains that he was out in the maelstrom of his time, acting, speaking, working and keeping the edges of his alert faith keen and cutting.

Dr. Ross Sanderson emphasizes this need of rethinking life in the terms of our congregation's existence: "Twenty-five years ago, Professor H. Richard Niebuhr saw that 'the religiously neglected poor, who fashion a new type of Christianity which corresponds to their distinctive needs, are likely to arise in the economic scale under the influence of religious discipline, and . . . in the midst of a freshly acquired cultural respectability, neglect the new poor succeeding them on the lower plane.' And, he records, Wesley himself faultlessly described the process whereby other churches of the disinherited, and his own with them, sloughed off their original character. 'Wherever riches have increased,' he wrote, 'the essence of religion has decreased in the same proportion. Therefore, I do not see how it is possible in the nature of things for any revival of religion to continue for long. For religion must necessarily produce both industry and frugality, and these cannot but produce riches.' " [8]

So, we are forever rethinking our faith. It is much like swimming the Niagara River. We are never done with it. Once we stop, we are over the falls. As we incarnate in our own midst a sensitive, adventurous Christian faith, we bring to bear upon the minds and lives of young people the essential integrity of a faith and its demands upon the total self.

Once, I interviewed a picket who was marching with his sign in front of the White House. He was against war. He wanted nothing to do with it at all. I asked him why he walked there and he assured me that he knew the President was in Warm Springs; that the President couldn't see his sign, but he wanted to register. Is this all the church can do? Are we simply to register a point of view, or are we to plead for a verdict? If we are to do the latter, then we shall recapture the imagination of young people and enable them to possess the heritage of faith which they received from their fathers and which they must now rethink in the terms of their social situations.

This is the problem Jesus confronted, and all of this sends us back to the Master preaching to his followers. "Ye have heard it said of old time," he counsels, "but I say unto you." Thus he places his finger on that which has caused his hearers to wince through the centuries. For he put it on the heart of the matter, the conscience of the matter, insisting that we are to be more than mere keepers of an outer code—that we are to be, rather, disciples of an inner compulsion. We are not to be content with the outward show of things, but strivers for the meaning of things. We are not to be tuned to the voice of society, but to the Word of God. Our religious life is not to be a campaign platform so much as a daily way of life. This faith is not an opinion

[8] R. W. Sanderson, *The Church Serves the Changing City* (New York: Harper, 1955), p. 18.

that we hold. It is an idea that possesses us. We are to be Christians plus.

The reader may well ask "After confirmation, what?" We are forever thrown back on interpreting the compelling Word of God in each new situation. That church is a living expression of the Word and Sacraments where maturing young minds and enthusiastic activists are at home, alive and alert to the compulsions and power of this faith. To rely on a single step such as the rite of confirmation is to deny the very lifeblood of that experience. "Stir up the gift that is in thee," implored Paul of Timothy. The church which claims Jesus Christ as its chief cornerstone must forever be alive. When it sends young people into the world with a new awareness of the power of the Word, it can be unafraid even though it will always be astonished. For what is so surprising as the Word become flesh and alive in our midst!

SOME SUGGESTIONS FROM OTHERS

Several pastors report that they have found their finest experiences with growing minds in rethinking articles of faith. For instance, one pastor has a group of high school seniors who are introduced to a study book such as "We Believe" by William Larsen and published by the Division of Student Service, National Lutheran Council. There are numerous other such surveys of Christian truth.

One pastor, spurred by the statement of Edward R. Murrow that so many persons had never actually written down what they believed, invited young married couples of his parish to an evening study group. They met one evening, talked over the matter and tried to write for themselves a brief statement of their faith. They then spent several weeks re-exploring the elements of historic Christianity, returning in the end to look again at what they had originally written. He reports that their studies had great meaning in personal faith as well as in his own preaching.

One pastor reports that he believes most problems which young people deal with are not intellectual difficulties, but moral ones. He has tried to attack the problem of the articles of their faith by the highway of their personal lives, their acknowledgment of sin, their understanding of the need of personal surrender. He believes passionately that most of his growing young men and women have needed greater guidance in this area than in any other.

Type used in this book
Body, 10 on 13 and 9 on 11 Janson
Display, Garamond